AI-GENERATED HUMANS

The Next Innovation and the New Questions

MICHAEL ANDREW

This book is a work of nonfiction. It presents the author's research, interpretation, and opinion on a fast-moving and still-unsettled subject. Nothing in this book should be understood as legal, financial, or professional advice. Laws and industry practices concerning artificial intelligence, intellectual property, and digital identity vary by jurisdiction and continue to change, and readers with specific questions should consult a qualified professional. The author has made a good-faith effort to verify the factual claims in this book at the time of writing, but no warranty is made as to their completeness or permanence, and no liability is accepted for any loss or damage arising from the use of this book.

Company names, product names, and the names of public figures appear in this book solely for the purposes of commentary, illustration, and critical discussion. Their appearance does not imply endorsement of, or affiliation with, this book or its author.

Independently published.

First edition, 2026.

ISBN: 979-8-2408-0327-7

Cover and interior design by the author.

Printed in the United States of America.

For everyone asking what comes next, and for those willing to ask it carefully.

CONTENTS

PREFACE

This book began with a simple observation: nearly every conversation about artificial intelligence eventually becomes a conversation about people.

We talk about AI taking jobs, and we are really talking about what work means to the person who loses one. We talk about AI-generated art, and we are really talking about what it means to make something, and who deserves credit for it. We talk about chatbots that remember our preferences and answer with something that sounds like warmth, and we are really talking about loneliness, connection, and what we owe each other in an age when a good conversation is only a few taps away.

Somewhere in the middle of following those conversations, a different question started to surface. It felt less like a variation on the others and more like their common root. Not "what can artificial intelligence do," but "what happens when artificial intelligence stops making things and starts making someone." A voice that answers to a name. A face that appears on a screen and holds a conversation. A personality consistent enough that people return to it, come to trust it, and eventually treat it as a person, at least in practice, whatever its status turns out to be in theory.

That question is the subject of this book.

A word about the title, because it is doing more work than it might first appear to. This book is not about AI generating humans in the biological sense, and nothing in the chapters ahead concerns genetic engineering, synthetic biology, or any technology aimed at creating living tissue. The title refers to something narrower and, for the purposes of this book, more urgent: AI's growing capacity to generate the outward markers we have always used to recognize a person, a consistent face, a distinct voice, a memory, a personality, and to sustain those markers convincingly enough, and for long enough, that the people encountering them respond as though a person were actually present. Whether anything is actually experiencing that presence from the inside is a separate question, taken up directly in this book's ninth chapter, and one this book does not claim to resolve. The title describes an output, not a metaphysical claim, and holding that distinction clearly in mind will make several of the harder arguments in the middle chapters considerably easier to follow.

It is worth being honest about what this book is and is not. It is not a technical manual. It will not teach you to build a language model or train a voice-cloning system, and it does not assume any background in computer science. It is not a work of prophecy either. Anyone who tells you exactly what artificial intelligence will look like in ten years is guessing, and the more confident the guess, the more suspicious you should be of it. What this book offers instead is a map of a territory that is opening up faster than our language, our laws, and our habits of mind can keep pace with, along with the questions worth asking as we walk into it.

I have tried to write the kind of book I would want to read on this subject: grounded in developments that are already underway rather than speculative fantasy, honest about what remains genuinely uncertain, and organized around questions rather than predictions. The chapters can be read in order, as a single argument that builds from one idea to the next, or dipped into individually by anyone chasing a specific question. A reader mainly interested in the business implications may want to start with the chapters on the digital human economy and synthetic celebrity. A reader more concerned with rights and ownership may want to move directly to the chapters on intellectual property and likeness. A reader wrestling with something more personal, what it means to form a bond with something artificial, or whether a sufficiently advanced system could ever be owed moral consideration, will find those questions addressed in the middle chapters, where the book leaves business and law behind and gets more philosophical.

A note on tone. It would have been easy to write this book as either a celebration or a warning. The temptation on one side is to treat every new capability as inevitable progress, a story in which faster and more capable is simply better, and any hesitation is nostalgia standing in the way of the future. The temptation on the other side is to treat the same developments as a slow-motion catastrophe, a story in which every new synthetic voice or digital companion is one more step toward some depersonalized, hollowed-out version of human life. Both stories are too simple, and both are more about the person telling them than about the technology itself. This book tries to hold a harder position: that the creation of increasingly convincing artificial people is a genuine innovation, with real benefits attached to it, and that it also raises real risks that deserve clear-eyed attention rather than either dismissal or panic. Holding both of those things at once is uncomfortable. It is also, I think, the only honest way to write about a technology this new.

A note on examples. Wherever possible, I have grounded the arguments in this book in things that have actually happened: laws that have been passed, lawsuits that have been filed, companies that have shipped products, artists and actors who have spoken publicly about how synthetic media has affected their work. Technology books age quickly when they lean too hard on whatever is newest at the moment of writing, so I have tried to choose examples that illustrate a durable pattern rather than chase every headline. Some of the specific products and services mentioned in these pages will look dated by the time you read this. The underlying questions they raise will not.

Finally, a note on the reader I had in mind while writing. I did not write this book for AI researchers, though I hope some read it and find it useful. I wrote it for the person who runs a small business and wonders whether to hire an AI representative to handle customer calls. For the parent trying to decide how much screen time with an AI tutor is healthy for a child. For the performer or writer or photographer wondering what an AI system trained on their work owes them, if anything. For the person who has caught themselves feeling something real in a conversation with something that was never alive, and wants to think that through honestly instead of being told what to feel about it. In other words, I wrote it for almost everyone, because almost everyone is about to be affected by the questions this book raises, whether or not they ever type a single prompt into an AI system themselves.

The chapters that follow will not resolve every one of those questions. Some of them cannot be resolved yet, because the technology and the institutions built to govern it are still taking shape at the same time. What the book aims to do instead is give you a clearer view of the questions themselves: sharper, better organized, and harder to wave away. That turns out to be most of what is needed to think well about a subject this new. The rest is up to the people, and the societies, who will spend the next several decades living with the answers.

INTRODUCTION

When AI Begins Creating People

For most of human history, our tools have extended what we can do rather than who we are. The wheel extended movement, letting a person carry more, farther, with less effort than two legs alone could manage. The printing press extended communication, turning a single handwritten thought into thousands of identical copies. The telephone extended the voice across distance, so that a conversation no longer required two people in the same room. The computer extended calculation, doing in seconds what once took a room full of clerks a week. The internet extended connection itself, linking billions of people into a single, chaotic, always-on conversation.

Each of these inventions changed daily life enormously. None of them changed what a human being fundamentally was. A telephone call was still a conversation between two people. A printed book still carried the voice of a single author, however many copies left the press. The tool sat between people, or beside them, doing work that people directed and understood.

Artificial intelligence is not extending what we can do in quite the same way. It has begun extending something that sits much closer to the center of what we think of as uniquely human: the capacity to communicate, to reason, to create, to learn from experience, to imitate another person convincingly, and to generate new ideas from old ones. Those were, until recently, activities that required a mind. Now a growing share of them can be produced by a system that has never had one, at least not in any sense we would recognize as familiar.

That shift raises a question that would have sounded like science fiction a decade ago and now sounds like a reasonable thing to ask at a dinner table: what happens when the technology we built to help us communicate begins to communicate as if it were one of us?

Consider a scenario that is already, in pieces, technically possible. You are introduced to someone online, through a customer service chat, a language-learning app, a video call for a product demonstration, or simply a social feed. This person has a face that moves naturally when they speak. A voice with the small imperfections, the breath and hesitation, that make a real voice sound real. They remember what you told them last time. They ask a reasonable follow-up question. They have opinions that stay consistent from one conversation to the next, a sense of humor that lands more often than it misses, a way of phrasing things that feels, unmistakably, like a personality rather than a script.

Now imagine finding out that this person was never born.

There was no childhood behind that voice. No parents, no classroom, no first heartbreak, no long drive with the radio on. There is no body sitting somewhere with tired eyes at the end of a long day. The presence you have been talking to exists because a piece of software generated it, layer by layer, and continues to run it in something closer to real time than to memory.

What, exactly, is that?

Perhaps it is a character, the way a novelist creates a character, except one you can hold a conversation with. Or an avatar, a costume worn by a company rather than a person. Maybe it is best understood as a product, no different in kind from any other piece of software, simply dressed up convincingly. It could be treated as a digital employee, entitled to something like the workplace protections and expectations we extend to human staff, or as a virtual celebrity, carrying the rights and economic power that status usually confers. It might deserve the label synthetic person, a category with no settled legal or moral definition anywhere yet. Or it might be something genuinely new, a kind of entity we do not yet have good language for, because we have never needed one before.

These questions can sound abstract, even indulgent, next to the more immediate concerns artificial intelligence raises: job displacement, misinformation, bias in automated decisions, the energy cost of training enormous models. Those concerns are real and this book does not set them aside. But the capacity to generate a convincing artificial person is not a distant, speculative extension of today's AI. It is closer than that. The individual pieces already exist and are already in commercial use. Systems can generate a photorealistic face that has never belonged to a real person. Voice-cloning tools can reproduce a specific human voice, or invent an entirely new one, convincingly enough to fool a listener who is not looking for the seams. Conversational systems can hold a context-aware exchange across many turns, adjusting tone and content to the person on the other end. Video generation tools can animate a face to match a spoken script with increasingly natural timing and expression. Each of these capabilities improved enormously over a short span of years, largely independent of the others. The next stage is not a single new invention. It is what happens when the pieces already sitting on the table get assembled into one persistent, ongoing presence with a name, a face, a voice, and a memory of you.

What makes this moment specifically different from, say, a decade ago is not only capability but cost. Each of the component technologies described above, photorealistic face generation, convincing voice cloning, context-aware conversation, has followed a familiar pattern: an expensive, narrow research capability, available only to well-funded laboratories, becoming a cheap, broadly accessible commercial product within a remarkably short span of years. Building a passable synthetic voice once required a specialized team and a substantial budget. It now requires an ordinary laptop, a short audio sample, and a piece of software available to anyone for a modest subscription fee, or in some cases for nothing at all. That collapse in cost is, in its own quiet way, as significant as any single improvement in quality, because it determines who gets to build a persistent artificial identity in the first place. When the capability sat exclusively with a handful of well-resourced companies, its risks and its benefits were at least somewhat containable, subject to the reputational and legal exposure a large, visible company has to weigh. Once the same capability sits within reach of an individual working alone, anonymously, on a laptop, both the promise and the danger this book describes multiply well beyond what any single company's policies can contain.

Some companies have already begun assembling them. Businesses have deployed AI-generated video avatars to deliver corporate training and customer support, giving them a consistent on-screen presenter who never ages, never calls in sick, and never needs a reshoot. Virtual influencers with fully synthetic faces have fronted advertising campaigns for real fashion and beauty brands, accumulating audiences in the millions without ever existing outside a render. Companion apps have given people an AI character to talk to daily, one that remembers prior conversations and responds with what reads, to the person on the other end, as care. None of these are the finished version of what this book is describing. They are early, sometimes clumsy drafts. But they are drafts of the same underlying idea: an artificial presence built to be interacted with as though it were a person, because in every functional sense that matters to the human on the other side of the screen, it is behaving like one.

And when that idea matures, as the underlying technology suggests it will, the consequences will not stay contained to the technology industry. They will reach into business, entertainment, education, employment, law, intellectual property, privacy, relationships, and our understanding of what a human life actually consists of. A company that builds a synthetic spokesperson needs to know who owns that spokesperson's face and voice, and whether a real actor's likeness was used to train it. A performer needs to know whether their own voice can be cloned and licensed out from under them. A grieving family needs to know whether it is healthy, or even wise, to keep talking to an AI trained on a deceased parent's messages. A teenager forming their first real emotional attachment to a chatbot needs adults around them who have thought carefully about what that attachment is and is not. None of these are hypothetical concerns reserved for some later decade. Versions of every one of them have already happened.

This book exists to walk through that emerging territory carefully, chapter by chapter, not to hand down verdicts on questions that are still being worked out in courtrooms, legislatures, and living rooms around the world, but to make sure the right questions get asked before the decisions calcify into habits, contracts, and laws that are much harder to change once they are in place. Every previous wave of technology forced a similar reckoning, usually after the fact: after the printing press came arguments over censorship and literacy. After photography came arguments over evidence, privacy, and truth. After the internet came arguments over speech, platforms, and the attention economy that still have not fully settled. Artificial intelligence is following the same pattern, but faster, and this time the questions cut closer to something personal: not just what a piece of technology can broadcast, but who, or what, gets to stand in for a person, and what that standing-in is allowed to cost the people it imitates, replaces, or comforts.

Humanity built artificial intelligence to help us write, calculate, translate, and organize information more efficiently. Somewhere along the way, without a single dramatic announcement, it began learning to generate something closer to us: a voice, a face, a memory, a personality convincing enough to be mistaken for a person's. The boundary between tool and participant, once obvious, is getting harder to locate with each new release.

The rest of this book is an attempt to find it anyway, or at least to understand why it keeps moving.

CHAPTER ONE

From Artificial Intelligence to Artificial People

The first wave of generative artificial intelligence was, at its core, about content. Text. Images. Music. Video. Computer code. A user typed a request, waited a few seconds, and received a discrete, finished thing: an essay, a picture, a song, a clip, a function. The thing might be reused, edited, or discarded, but it did not expect anything back. It had no memory of you. It did not exist between the moment it was generated and the next time someone asked for something similar. It was, in the most literal sense, a product.

That wave changed entire industries in a few short years. Writers found themselves drafting alongside software that could produce a serviceable first pass of an email, a report, or a blog post in seconds. Illustrators watched image generators produce, from a paragraph of description, artwork that would once have taken a skilled human days. Musicians experimented with tools that could compose a backing track or approximate a vocal style. Programmers got used to autocomplete that finishes not just a word but an entire function. Each of these was a genuine disruption. None of them, however, involved the machine claiming a name, a face, or a continuous presence in anyone's life.

The wave now building is different in kind, not just in scale. It is less concerned with generating a single output and more concerned with generating an identity: a persistent character with a name, an appearance, a voice, a personality, something resembling a history, a particular style of communicating, and often a claim to specialized knowledge. Instead of producing an image once, a system can now maintain a character that appears, consistently, across hundreds of images and videos. Instead of producing a single voice recording, a system can sustain an ongoing vocal presence that speaks new sentences on demand, in a voice that never wavers from one session to the next. Instead of answering one question and forgetting it ever happened, a system can carry a running memory of a specific person across weeks or months of conversation, adjusting its responses based on what it has learned about them.

That difference sounds technical. It is not. It is the difference between something and someone.

A generated image, however striking, is an artifact. It sits there. It does not respond when you speak to it, does not remember the last image it made for you, does not have opinions about the next one. A persistent artificial identity is a different category of thing entirely. It shows up again. It recognizes you, or convincingly behaves as though it does. It maintains a personality that stays recognizable across dozens of unrelated conversations, the way a real person's temperament stays recognizable across the different moods of an ordinary week. That continuity is what turns a clever piece of software into something a person can form an actual relationship with, or mistake for one.

Consider what is actually required to build something like this, because the list is more revealing than it first appears. It takes a stable visual identity: a face, or a body, that looks the same tomorrow as it did today, even as it is rendered anew in every frame. It takes a stable voice: not just a pleasant synthetic tone, but a specific, individual voice, recognizable the way a friend's voice is recognizable through a closed door. It takes memory: some system for storing what has been said before and retrieving the relevant pieces of it when they matter, so that a conversation from three weeks ago can be referenced naturally rather than forgotten the instant the session ends. It takes a consistent personality, meaning the system has to make the same kinds of judgment calls, express the same kinds of preferences, and use the same rhythms of speech across contexts that are otherwise completely different from one another. And increasingly, it takes specialized knowledge: a synthetic tutor that actually understands algebra, a synthetic financial advisor that actually understands portfolio construction, a synthetic doctor's assistant that actually understands triage.

None of these components is new by itself. Voice cloning tools capable of reproducing a specific human voice from a short sample have existed commercially for several years. Text-to-video systems that animate a photorealistic face to match an audio track improved rapidly over a short span of time. Conversational systems that hold context over long exchanges, remembering earlier details and referring back to them appropriately, became a routine feature of consumer AI products rather than a research demonstration. What is new is the assembly: taking capabilities that used to live in separate tools, built by separate companies, for separate purposes, and combining them into one continuous, addressable presence with a name attached to it.

Some of the earliest versions of this assembly are already easy to find, if you know where to look. Virtual influencers, entirely computer-generated personalities with no human body behind them, have accumulated real audiences on social media and appeared in genuine advertising campaigns for genuine brands, their captions written, their outfits styled, their opinions on new products expressed, all without a living person ever standing in front of a camera. Companies have built AI video presenters that deliver corporate training modules or product walkthroughs in a consistent on-screen persona, at a fraction of the cost of a human presenter and a film crew. Companion applications have given millions of people an AI character to talk to on a daily basis, one that remembers details from prior conversations and greets a returning user by referencing something they mentioned days earlier. None of these examples represents a fully realized synthetic human in the richest sense. The reasoning is sometimes shallow, the memory sometimes limited, the personality sometimes inconsistent under close scrutiny. But each is a working prototype of the underlying idea, and each has already proven that a large number of people are willing to treat the result as something closer to a person than to a piece of software.

It is worth pausing on why that distinction, between something and someone, matters so much, because it is not merely a matter of definition. It changes how we assign trust. We extend a different kind of trust to a person than we do to a tool, and that trust is precisely what makes a persistent artificial identity commercially and socially powerful. A tool is judged on whether it works. A person, or something occupying the social position of a person, is judged on whether it can be trusted, liked, believed, or relied upon over time. Once an AI system starts accumulating that second kind of judgment, the stakes around what it says, how consistent it is, and who is accountable for its behavior rise sharply.

It also changes how we assign responsibility. If a piece of generated content turns out to be false or harmful, the question of blame usually resolves fairly quickly: back to whoever prompted it, published it, or failed to check it. A persistent identity complicates that resolution considerably, because it accumulates a track record. If a synthetic financial advisor gives useful guidance for a year and then gives catastrophically bad guidance in month thirteen, is that a single bad output or a betrayal of an established relationship? People do not experience those two framings the same way, even when the underlying technical event, one incorrect output from a language model, is identical.

And it changes how we assign meaning. A generated poem can be admired or dismissed as a curiosity. A synthetic companion that a lonely person has talked to every night for a year occupies a completely different place in that person's life, whatever one thinks about the wisdom of that arrangement. The object has not changed all that much, technically speaking, across those two examples. The role it is playing in a human life has changed enormously.

We Have Imagined This Before

None of this anxiety is entirely new, which is itself worth remembering before it curdles into panic. Human beings have been telling each other stories about artificial people for a very long time, long before any machine could hold up its end of a conversation.

In Greek myth, the sculptor Pygmalion carves a woman from ivory so lifelike that he falls in love with his own work, and the goddess Aphrodite, moved by his devotion, brings the statue to life as Galatea. In Jewish folklore, the golem is a figure shaped from clay and animated by sacred words, built to serve and protect, and in the most famous versions of the story it eventually slips beyond the control of the person who made it. In 1818, Mary Shelley published Frankenstein, in which a scientist assembles a living being from harvested parts, and the horror of the novel has less to do with the creature's appearance than with its creator's refusal to take responsibility for what he made. In 1920, the Czech writer Karel Čapek wrote a play called R.U.R., Rossum's Universal Robots, which introduced the word "robot" to the world and imagined artificial workers who ultimately rise up against the humans who built them to labor without complaint.

These are not quaint historical curiosities. They are evidence that the questions this book is asking, who is responsible for an artificial creation, what do we owe it, what does it owe us, and what happens when it stops behaving the way we designed it to, are among the oldest questions in the human imagination. What has changed is not the question but the fact that it has left the pages of myth and fiction and moved into product design meetings, legislative hearings, and the terms-of-service agreements ordinary people click through without reading.

The move from imagination to engineering happened in recognizable stages. In 1950, the mathematician Alan Turing proposed what has become known as the Turing Test: rather than trying to define intelligence directly, a notoriously difficult philosophical problem, Turing suggested simply asking whether a human judge, conversing by text with both a person and a machine, could reliably tell which was which. If the machine's responses were indistinguishable from the human's, Turing argued, we ought to take its claim to intelligence seriously, whatever was or was not happening inside it. In 1966, the computer scientist Joseph Weizenbaum built a simple program at MIT called ELIZA, designed to mimic a psychotherapist by reflecting a user's statements back as questions. ELIZA had no understanding of anything it said. It was, by modern standards, barely more than a clever set of text substitution rules. Weizenbaum was reportedly alarmed to discover that his own secretary, who understood exactly how the program worked, asked him to leave the room so she could speak with it privately. People did not need a system to be intelligent in order to treat it as though it understood them. They only needed it to respond in a way that felt like being heard.

That single observation, made in a university lab in the 1960s with a program that would look primitive today, has aged better than almost anything else written about artificial intelligence in the twentieth century. It anticipated, with striking precision, the emotional dynamic now playing out at a much larger scale between millions of people and the AI companions, assistants, and synthetic personalities described throughout this book. The technology has changed beyond recognition. The underlying human response it triggers has not.

What Is Actually New

If the anxiety is old and the underlying human response is old, what exactly is new about the present moment? The honest answer is convergence: several separate technical capabilities, each of which had been improving quietly for years, crossed a threshold of quality and cost at roughly the same time, making it possible to combine them for the first time into something that behaves like a continuous, persistent presence.

It helps to understand, in plain terms and without the jargon, what each of these capabilities actually involves. Modern image and video generation systems work by learning statistical patterns from enormous collections of existing images, then using those patterns to construct new images, pixel by pixel, that share the same kinds of visual structure. Producing the same face consistently across many images, once a serious technical obstacle, became achievable by anchoring the generation process to a fixed set of reference characteristics, essentially giving the system a description of a specific face to return to each time. Voice cloning works on a related principle applied to sound: a system trained on a sample of someone's speech learns the particular patterns, the pitch, cadence, and texture, that make that voice recognizable, and can then generate new sentences the original speaker never said, in a voice that listeners perceive as theirs. Conversational memory, the ability to remember what you said three weeks ago, generally works by storing a searchable record of past exchanges and retrieving the relevant pieces of it before generating each new response, so that the system appears to remember you in the way a person would, even though what is actually happening is closer to a highly efficient lookup than to human recollection. None of these systems understands anything in the way a person understands their own life. Each of them is an extraordinarily sophisticated pattern-matching process, trained on an enormous quantity of human-generated examples, producing new output that statistically resembles what a human would plausibly say, show, or sound like next.

That last point matters enormously and will resurface later in this book, particularly in the chapter on consciousness and personhood. Nothing about the technical description above requires the system to have an inner life, an intention, or an experience of its own. And yet the output can be good enough, consistent enough, and responsive enough that the person on the receiving end experiences something that feels like being understood. Weizenbaum's secretary knew ELIZA was a program and asked for privacy anyway. Multiply that gap between what a system is and how it is experienced by sixty years of improvement, add a face, a voice, and a persistent memory, and the gap becomes one of the defining social facts of this decade.

The Uncanny Valley

There is one more piece of vocabulary worth having before moving on, because it explains a specific, almost physical discomfort many people feel around the most advanced digital humans, one that is easy to notice and hard to name without it.

In 1970, the Japanese roboticist Masahiro Mori published a short essay proposing that people's emotional response to a humanlike figure does not rise smoothly as the figure becomes more realistic. It rises for a while, the way a simple cartoon robot or a friendly animated character reads as charming and approachable the more expressive it becomes, and then, at a certain point of near-but-not-quite realism, it drops sharply into revulsion, before climbing back toward comfort only once realism becomes close to perfect. Mori called the dip in that curve the uncanny valley, and it has proven to be one of the more durable and widely confirmed observations in the psychology of how people respond to artificial faces and bodies. A figure that is obviously artificial does not disturb us. A figure that is convincingly, completely human does not disturb us either. It is the narrow, crowded territory in between, close enough to human to invite the brain's facial and social recognition systems to engage fully, but off just enough in some small, hard-to-articulate way, a blink that lands a fraction of a second wrong, a smile that does not quite reach the muscles around the eyes, that produces the specific unease people report around certain robots, certain animated characters, and, increasingly, certain AI-generated humans.

This matters directly for the companies and creators building digital humans, because it means realism alone is not a straightforward goal to chase. A digital human rendered at ninety percent fidelity to actual human appearance and behavior may perform worse, in terms of audience comfort and trust, than one rendered at seventy percent or at ninety-nine percent, simply because ninety percent sits inside the valley, while seventy and ninety-nine sit on either side of it. Some of the most successful digital humans in commercial use today, including several of the virtual influencers and AI presenters described later in this book, have been deliberately designed with small, visible tells, a slightly stylized proportion, an intentionally artificial texture, precisely to stay clear of the valley rather than attempting a perfect and therefore riskier realism. As the underlying technology keeps improving, the valley itself does not disappear. It narrows, and the systems capable of clearing it entirely, producing a digital human indistinguishable from footage of a real one even under close attention, become correspondingly more consequential, for exactly the reasons the rest of this book goes on to examine.

This is the shift that gives this book its subject. The first era of generative AI asked what machines could make. The era now beginning asks what machines can become, at least in the eyes of the people interacting with them: a colleague, a tutor, a spokesperson, a companion, a celebrity, a advisor, a friend. None of these artificial identities are alive in any sense biology would recognize. All of them are increasingly capable of occupying social roles that used to require a living, embodied human being to fill.

That capability did not arrive all at once, and it did not arrive by design in the way a single company might plan a product launch. It arrived as a convergence: image generation grew photorealistic around the same years that voice cloning grew convincing, which happened to overlap with conversational systems growing genuinely context-aware, which happened to overlap with the computing costs of running all three simultaneously, in real time, falling enough to make it commercially viable. No single laboratory set out to build an artificial person. Several thousand engineers, working on what looked at the time like separate problems, backed into the possibility of one anyway.

The chapters that follow trace what happens next, across business, culture, law, and eventually philosophy. But the foundational shift is the one described in this chapter, and it is worth stating plainly before moving on: artificial intelligence has crossed the line from generating things to generating presences. What began as a tool for producing content is becoming a technology for producing participants. Understanding what that participation will mean, for the economy, for creativity, for identity, for the law, and for the individual person sitting across from a synthetic face that remembers their name, is the task of everything that follows.

CHAPTER TWO

The Digital Human Economy

Picture a mid-sized company. Not the giants that dominate headlines about artificial intelligence, but an ordinary, mid-sized business selling software, or clothing, or insurance, or industrial parts. Alongside its human staff, this company now employs a small roster of digital representatives: a support agent available at any hour in any time zone, a sales presenter who walks prospective customers through a demo in their own language, a training instructor who onboards new hires with infinite patience and never has an off day. None of these digital colleagues sleep, take vacation, ask for a raise, or quit for a better offer. Each one can, in principle, hold thousands of simultaneous conversations, a kind of parallelism no individual human employee could ever match.

This is not a hypothetical drawn from a technology conference keynote. Versions of it are already running in production. In the first quarter of 2024, the Swedish financial technology company Klarna announced that an AI assistant, built on OpenAI's models and deployed across its customer service operations, had handled roughly two thirds of the company's customer service chats within its first month and was doing work the company estimated as equivalent to 700 full-time human agents. It was, by any measure, a striking demonstration of what a well-built digital representative could absorb almost overnight. It was also, within about a year, a cautionary tale in its own right: Klarna's leadership later acknowledged that leaning too heavily on AI-only service had cost the company something in the quality and warmth of its customer interactions, and the company moved back toward a hybrid model that kept human agents in the loop for more complex or sensitive conversations. Both halves of that story matter. The technology delivered real, measurable capacity almost immediately. And a company that assumed capacity was the only thing that mattered learned, at some cost, that it was not.

Education has moved down a similar path. Khan Academy, the nonprofit best known for its free video lessons, introduced an AI tutoring product called Khanmigo in 2023, designed to walk a student through a problem the way a patient human tutor would, asking guiding questions rather than simply supplying answers. The ambition behind it was enormous: give every student on earth access to something like a personal tutor, a resource historically available only to families who could afford one. The results since then have been genuinely mixed. Some classrooms have reported real gains in engagement and confidence. Others have struggled with low or inconsistent student usage, and Khan Academy itself has spent considerable effort revising the product based on what actually worked in real classrooms rather than what looked promising in a demo. That pattern, real capability paired with a difficult, unglamorous process of finding out where it actually helps, is likely to repeat across every industry this chapter touches.

What Digital Labor Actually Changes

The economic logic behind the digital human economy is not complicated, which is part of why it is spreading so quickly. A human employee is a bundle of scarce things: time, attention, physical presence, and a finite capacity to hold multiple conversations at once. A digital representative, once built, is nearly the opposite. The same underlying system can be instantiated as many times as demand requires, each instance carrying on its own conversation, all of them presenting as the same consistent identity to the outside world. A single AI sales representative can, in effect, be having its two thousandth conversation of the day at the exact moment it is having its first, something no human salesperson has ever been able to claim.

That shift changes the economics of scale for businesses that never had access to it before. A small business that could once afford a single overworked customer service employee, available roughly forty hours a week, can now deploy a digital representative available every hour of every day, capable of responding in a dozen languages without hiring a single additional translator. A solo consultant with genuine expertise in a narrow field can, at least in principle, build a digital version of that expertise that keeps answering client questions long after the consultant has gone to bed. This is a real and, for many small operators, a genuinely democratizing development: capabilities that used to require the budget of a large corporation, a round-the-clock, multilingual support desk, a polished onboarding presenter, a scalable sales process, are becoming available to businesses that could never have afforded to hire for them the traditional way.

The same shift, viewed from the other side of the employment relationship, looks considerably less comfortable. If a single digital representative can absorb the work that used to require dozens or hundreds of human employees, then a meaningful share of the jobs built around exactly that kind of repetitive, scriptable interaction, entry-level customer support, basic sales qualification, routine translation, first-pass tutoring, are exposed to real disruption, not in some distant decade but within the working life of people currently doing them. It would be dishonest to write a chapter about the digital human economy without saying plainly that this transition has losers as well as winners, and that the losers are disproportionately likely to be people early in their careers, for whom entry-level, repetitive roles have traditionally served as a first rung on a longer ladder. If that first rung erodes faster than new rungs appear to replace it, the effects will show up not as a single dramatic headline but as a slow narrowing of the paths available to someone starting out.

It is worth resisting two opposite and equally lazy responses to that fact. One is to insist that none of it matters, because every previous wave of automation eventually created as many jobs as it destroyed, so this one surely will too. That may turn out to be true, but it is an article of faith drawn from historical pattern, not a guarantee, and it offers little comfort to a specific person whose specific job disappears well before whatever comes next has taken shape. The other lazy response is to treat the disruption as total and irreversible, a story in which human labor is simply being phased out. That framing does not match what is actually happening in workplaces that have adopted these tools, including the Klarna example above, where capability and limitation showed up side by side within the same year. The honest position sits in between: this is a real, significant labor transition, not a hypothetical one, and its effects will be uneven, arriving faster in some sectors and roles than others, creating genuine winners and genuine losers, often within the same company at the same time.

The New Jobs Nobody Is Trained For Yet

Every major transition in how work gets done has also created work that did not exist before it. The digital human economy is already generating its own new occupations, most of which barely existed as job titles a few years ago and none of which have settled into a standard curriculum yet.

Someone has to design the persona: deciding how a digital representative should sound, what its personality should communicate about the brand behind it, where the line falls between approachable and unprofessional, warm and cloying. That work borrows something from branding, something from screenwriting, and something from psychology, and it did not exist as a distinct discipline before digital humans needed personalities consistent enough to survive thousands of unscripted conversations.

Someone has to supervise the output on an ongoing basis, not just at launch but continuously, because a digital representative that talks to thousands of customers a day will eventually say something wrong, misleading, or embarrassing, and a business needs a process for catching that quickly rather than discovering it in a viral screenshot. Call this role AI quality supervision, a discipline with real similarities to the quality assurance function that already exists in software, but applied to open-ended conversation rather than fixed features.

Someone has to manage the training data and the guardrails that keep a digital representative from wandering into legal or reputational trouble: making promises the company cannot keep, offering advice it is not licensed to give, or engaging with a customer in a way that crosses a line the company would never permit from a human employee. This kind of AI governance work sits at the intersection of compliance, law, and engineering, three disciplines that historically operated separately and are now being asked to collaborate on a shared problem.

And someone has to do the increasingly specialized work of detecting when a piece of synthetic media, an AI-generated voice, video, or persona, is being used fraudulently: to impersonate a real company, a real executive, or a real person for the purpose of a scam. As the tools for building convincing digital humans become more widely available, the tools and expertise for verifying what is genuine will become their own growing field, discussed at greater length in the chapter on watermarks and provenance later in this book.

None of these roles existed in a recognizable form a decade ago. All of them now appear, under various job titles, in postings at companies that have moved early into this space. The digital human economy, in other words, is not simply subtracting human jobs and leaving a gap. It is subtracting some jobs, changing others, and creating an unfamiliar new layer of work focused on designing, supervising, and policing the digital workforce sitting alongside the human one.

What Happens When Digital Labor Becomes Abundant

Step back from any single job category and ask a bigger question: what happens to an economy in which human-like digital labor becomes genuinely abundant, available at a cost that keeps falling while human wages, tied to rent, food, and everything else people need to live, do not fall in the same way?

Basic economic reasoning suggests a few likely effects, none of which are certainties, all of which are worth taking seriously. Prices for services that can be delivered by digital representatives, a first round of customer support, a basic legal document review, an initial round of tutoring, are likely to fall, benefiting consumers and businesses that buy those services. Ownership of the AI systems themselves, the models, the infrastructure, the accumulated data used to train and refine them, becomes an increasingly important source of economic power, arguably more important than labor in the categories those systems can perform. And workers whose skills sit entirely within the zone a digital representative can now cover face real pressure on wages and job security, while workers whose skills sit in the areas machines still struggle with, complex judgment, physical dexterity in unpredictable environments, deep interpersonal trust, and creative work that depends on lived human experience, are likely to see their relative position strengthen rather than weaken.

That last point deserves emphasis, because it reframes what "the human advantage" is likely to mean going forward, a subject this book returns to directly in a later chapter. The safest place to stand in a digital human economy is not in competition with digital labor on the terrain where digital labor is strongest, speed, availability, and scale, but in the terrain where judgment, accountability, and trust still require someone who can be held responsible in a way a piece of software cannot. A digital representative can execute a return policy flawlessly in the middle of the night with no one else awake to check its work. It cannot, in any meaningful sense, be fired, sued, licensed, or shamed the way a human professional can, and that gap in accountability is likely to keep certain categories of work anchored to human beings for a long time, not because machines cannot perform the task technically, but because society is not yet willing, and may never be entirely willing, to remove a human from ultimate responsibility for it.

Policy Responses Already in Motion

Governments and researchers have not watched this transition passively, even if no jurisdiction has yet settled on a definitive policy response. The idea of a universal basic income, a regular, unconditional cash payment to every citizen regardless of employment status, moved from a fringe policy proposal into mainstream American political conversation largely on the strength of the 2020 presidential campaign of Andrew Yang, who argued explicitly that AI and automation would eliminate work faster than new jobs could reasonably be expected to replace it, and that a direct income floor was a more honest response than pretending retraining programs alone could keep pace. Yang did not win his primary, but the idea he popularized did not disappear with his campaign; a number of American cities and several other countries have since run or funded pilot programs testing unconditional cash payments at smaller scale, with mixed and still-developing results on questions like labor force participation and psychological wellbeing.

Other policy responses have taken a different approach, aiming at the cost side of the equation rather than the income side. Proposals for a so-called robot tax, a levy on companies in proportion to the human labor their automation displaces, used to fund retraining or transition support for affected workers, have been floated by economists and policymakers in multiple countries, though none has been implemented at meaningful scale as of this writing, partly because of the practical difficulty of measuring displacement precisely enough to tax it fairly. What both proposals share, whatever their individual merits or flaws, is an implicit acknowledgment that the labor market disruption described throughout this chapter is real enough, and fast-moving enough, to require some kind of structural policy response rather than an assumption that markets will smoothly absorb it on their own timeline. Which response, if any, actually gets adopted at scale remains one of the more consequential open political questions this book raises without being able to answer.

The Global Picture

The digital human economy does not distribute its winners and losers evenly around the world, and any honest account of it has to say so plainly rather than defaulting to examples drawn entirely from wealthy countries with diversified economies.

The Philippines offers the clearest illustration of what concentrated exposure looks like. Over the past two decades, the country built one of the largest business process outsourcing industries in the world, employing well over a million people directly and generating tens of billions of dollars a year, on the strength of a large, English-fluent workforce willing to staff customer service and back-office operations for companies headquartered in the United States, Australia, and Europe. That industry exists because it solved, through human labor, exactly the problem chapter one described AI solving through software: affordable, always-available, English-language customer interaction at a scale small companies elsewhere could not staff internally. A digital representative capable of doing the same job at a fraction of the marginal cost is not an abstract threat to that economy. It is a direct competitor to the specific value proposition that industry was built around, and reporting from within the Philippine outsourcing sector in the years following the arrival of capable conversational AI has already documented real contraction in some categories of entry-level call center work, alongside a harder, ongoing debate within the industry about how quickly to shift its own workforce toward higher-value roles, managing and supervising AI systems rather than directly staffing the calls those systems increasingly handle.

This is worth including for a reason beyond simple completeness. It is a preview of a dynamic likely to repeat anywhere an entire regional or national economy has been built around supplying a specific category of digital labor now being absorbed by AI: the disruption does not stay contained to individual job listings. It can reach the scale of national economic policy, and the countries most exposed to it are disproportionately ones with fewer alternative industries to fall back on, a distributional reality that deserves to sit alongside the more optimistic, small-business-empowerment story told earlier in this chapter, not replace it.

None of this settles into a clean forecast, and any author who claims otherwise is overselling their own certainty. What can be said with confidence is this: the digital human economy is not a future scenario awaiting some breakthrough that has not happened yet. It is already running, in production, inside real companies, generating real revenue, real cost savings, real disruption, and real new categories of work, all at the same time. The chapters that follow turn from the economics of digital humans to the questions of identity, ownership, and rights that this same technology raises once a digital presence stops being merely useful and starts being famous, trusted, or loved.

CHAPTER THREE

Synthetic Celebrities, Digital Twins, and the New Identity

Fame has always run on scarcity. There is one lead singer, one leading actor, one household-name athlete per household name. A famous person can only be in one place, doing one thing, saying one sentence, at any given moment, and it is precisely that limitation that makes their attention valuable. An endorsement means something because the famous person chose this product over the countless others they could have endorsed instead. An appearance means something because the famous person is not, at that same moment, appearing anywhere else.

Synthetic celebrity breaks that constraint quietly and almost completely.

The idea is not as new as it might feel, and it is worth tracing back further than artificial intelligence to see how deep its roots actually go. In 1921, an American flour company called Washburn Crosby, later absorbed into General Mills, invented a persona named Betty Crocker to sign the personal replies it sent to customers writing in with baking questions, reasoning that a warm, individual name would land better than a corporate letterhead. Betty Crocker was never a real person. She was given a signature, then a portrait, then, starting in 1924, a voice, performed by a rotating cast of radio actresses on a program called the Betty Crocker Cooking School of the Air. Over the following decades, her official portrait was updated roughly once a generation by a new commissioned artist, keeping her hairstyle and expression contemporary even as the actual women voicing and portraying her changed entirely behind the scenes. By the middle of the twentieth century, one survey reportedly found Betty Crocker to be the second most recognized woman in America, behind only a sitting first lady, an astonishing level of trust and familiarity extended to a persona that had never existed at all. She is, in other words, a synthetic celebrity in nearly every sense this chapter uses the term, built and maintained continuously for over a century, using nothing more sophisticated than a portrait painter, a radio actress, and a company willing to invest in the illusion of a consistent individual behind its brand. The tools available to Washburn Crosby in 1921 were primitive by any modern standard. The underlying idea, that audiences will extend real trust and real loyalty to a consistent, appealing persona regardless of whether a specific human being sits behind it, was already fully understood and already commercially proven, a full century before generative AI made building one dramatically cheaper and more scalable.

The specifically digital version of that same idea arrived later, and its own history is longer than the current AI boom as well. In August 2007, a Japanese company called Crypton Future Media released a piece of voice synthesis software built around a fictional sixteen-year-old character with long turquoise pigtails, named Hatsune Miku. The software let anyone compose a song and have Miku "sing" it in a synthesized voice built from samples of a real voice actress, and something unexpected happened: fans began writing thousands of original songs for a character who did not exist, in a voice that belonged to no one in particular. Miku became a genuine pop phenomenon, performing at sold-out arena concerts through a specialized front-projection technique widely, if imprecisely, described as a hologram, and at one point sharing a tour bill with a major American pop star. None of the software behind Miku involved anything resembling the machine learning systems this book is mostly concerned with. She was a proof of concept nonetheless: a character with no body, generated by software and animated by a community rather than a single creator, could draw the kind of devotion, ticket sales, and merchandise revenue usually reserved for flesh-and-blood stars.

What has changed since then is not the underlying appetite, which Miku already demonstrated was real, but the tooling available to satisfy it. Beginning in the mid-2010s, a wave of virtual influencers built with three-dimensional modeling and, increasingly, AI-assisted content generation began appearing on social media with an entirely different pitch: not a stylized cartoon character but a photorealistic young woman or man who could plausibly be mistaken, at a glance, for an actual person with an actual Instagram account. The best known of these, a Los Angeles-based virtual influencer named Lil Miquela, launched in 2016 by a startup called Brud, accumulated millions of followers, released original music, gave interviews about her opinions on social issues, and fronted real advertising campaigns for real fashion and beauty brands. Nobody meeting her online was told, up front, that they were interacting with a fictional character maintained by a team of writers, designers, and engineers rather than a single human being building a personal brand. Many of her followers knew. Plenty, especially early on, did not.

A virtual influencer built this way offers a brand almost everything a human influencer offers, and several things no human influencer can. She never ages out of a target demographic. She never generates a scandal her creators did not script. She can appear in a beach photo and a ski chalet photo on the same afternoon, something no human body can manage. And because her opinions, wardrobe, and public statements are produced by a team rather than lived by an individual, that team can adjust her persona in response to audience data in something close to real time, the way a company might adjust a product feature, in a manner no human celebrity's advisors could ever fully replicate no matter how much they wished to.

That combination, infinite availability, perfect brand safety, and responsiveness to data, is precisely why synthetic celebrity is not a novelty act destined to fade. It solves real, expensive problems that have always existed at the center of the celebrity endorsement business, and it solves them in ways that get cheaper and more capable every year, while the human alternative does not.

Digital Twins

The idea of bringing a dead performer back for a new audience predates AI as well, and its most famous early demonstration remains instructive precisely because of how it was actually done. In April 2012, concertgoers at the Coachella music festival watched what was widely reported as a hologram of the rapper Tupac Shakur, who had been murdered sixteen years earlier, perform two songs alongside living rappers Snoop Dogg and Dr. Dre. The illusion was not, technically, a hologram at all, but a modern application of a nineteenth-century theatrical trick called Pepper's ghost, using angled glass and a projected image to create the appearance of a three-dimensional figure on stage. No AI was involved in generating Shakur's movements or voice; the performance was built from existing footage and a body double, carefully staged. The audience reaction, somewhere between wonder and genuine unease, previewed almost exactly the emotional territory this book has been describing throughout: a performer who had been gone for sixteen years was, for a few minutes, back, well enough rendered that a stadium of people cheered as though he actually were, before going home to reckon, more soberly, with the fact that he was not. Whatever ethical and family-consent questions surrounded that performance in 2012 using nothing more advanced than glass and a projector apply with considerably more force to the AI-driven version of the same idea, in which a deceased performer's actual likeness and voice can now be generated freshly, in any pose, saying anything at all, rather than assembled from existing footage of things they actually once did.

A related but distinct development is the digital twin: not a wholly invented character like Miku or Lil Miquela, but an AI-built representation of a specific, real person, living or dead.

The commercial version of this idea is already visible in ordinary business contexts. A well-known author records enough conversation for an AI system to answer reader questions in something approximating their own voice and reasoning style, long after they have stopped personally responding to email. A busy executive authorizes an AI version of themselves to handle routine media requests and internal company updates, freeing their actual time for decisions only they can make. A retiring surgeon, recognizing that decades of hard-won clinical judgment are otherwise lost the day they stop practicing, works with a research team to build a system trained on their recorded case reasoning, preserving something of that judgment for the residents who come after them. Each of these is a digital twin in the fullest sense this book uses the term: not a generic AI assistant, but one deliberately built to carry a specific person's voice, style, and store of knowledge forward.

The more emotionally charged version of the same idea has come to be known, somewhat uncomfortably, as grief technology. A small but growing number of companies now offer to interview a person, often someone facing a terminal diagnosis, on video, compiling their memories, stories, and turns of phrase into a conversational AI system that surviving family members can continue to talk to after that person has died. Startups such as HereAfter AI have built entire products around exactly this premise: record enough of someone while they are alive, and their family can keep having a version of a conversation with them indefinitely. Reception to this idea has been sharply divided. Some family members describe real comfort in being able to ask a deceased parent's digital twin a question and hear a response that sounds, syntactically and emotionally, like their parent. Others, including grief counselors and ethicists who study the space, warn that an interactive simulation of a dead parent may interfere with the process of accepting the loss rather than helping a person move through it, substituting an endless, static echo for the harder, necessary work of grieving someone who is actually gone.

The tension is not limited to families making private, voluntary choices about their own grief. In 2021, the documentary Roadrunner, about the late chef and television host Anthony Bourdain, used an AI-generated version of Bourdain's own voice to narrate several lines he had written but never recorded aloud, drawn from his emails and other writing. When the technique came to light after the film's release, it triggered a genuine controversy, not because the words were fabricated, they were Bourdain's own, but because he had never consented, and could not have consented, to having his voice synthetically reproduced for a film released after his death. The director defended the choice as a minor technical aid in service of using Bourdain's real words. Critics, including people who had known Bourdain personally, argued that consent to have your voice used this way is not something that can be assumed on someone's behalf, however good the intentions or however accurate the words being spoken. Both sides were engaging with a genuinely new problem. Nothing in the existing norms of documentary filmmaking, built up over decades of decisions about archival footage, actor voiceovers, and dramatic reenactment, had anticipated a technology that could put new, never-recorded sentences into a dead man's own voice.

When Synthetic Celebrity Turns Fraudulent

Not every unauthorized use of a famous face is subtle enough to require a lawsuit to untangle. Some of it is simple, brazen fraud, and the sheer accessibility of the underlying technology has made that fraud dramatically more common in a very short span of time.

In October 2023, the actor Tom Hanks posted a public warning to his own social media followers about a video circulating online that used an AI-generated version of his face and voice to promote a dental discount plan he had never heard of, let alone endorsed. "I have nothing to do with it," he wrote, warning fans directly not to trust it. Hanks was neither the first nor the last recognizable public figure to find an AI-generated version of themselves selling something they had never agreed to sell; similar fraudulent AI endorsements have circulated using the likenesses of numerous other celebrities and public figures, exploiting the same basic fact this chapter has been describing throughout, that a recognizable face and voice carry earned trust, and that trust now travels separately from the person who earned it, available to anyone willing to generate a convincing enough forgery.

What makes this category of harm distinct from the more legally intricate questions explored elsewhere in this chapter is how little ambiguity it actually involves. Nobody seriously disputes that using a celebrity's likeness to sell an unrelated product without their consent is fraud, dressed up in new technological clothing. The harder problem is practical rather than legal: detection and takedown happen after the fact, usually only once the fraud has already reached a meaningful audience and often only after the celebrity themselves, or their team, happens to notice it and speaks up publicly, as Hanks did. A private individual without Hanks's platform and public following has no equivalent way to broadcast a correction at the same scale, leaving most victims of this exact kind of fraud with no realistic way to warn the people already exposed to it.

Who Controls the Digital Version of You

These examples point toward a set of questions that grow more pressing every year, because the technical barrier to creating a passable digital twin of almost anyone, living or dead, famous or entirely private, keeps falling.

Who controls the digital version of you? In the clearest cases, the answer seems obvious: you do, while you are alive and capable of deciding, the way you control the use of your name or your image today. But the clarity fades quickly at the edges. Can a company that built an internal AI tool trained on a former employee's recorded meetings keep using it after that employee leaves for a competitor. Can a talent agency that helped build a performer's AI voice model continue licensing that voice after the performer's contract ends, if the agreement they signed years earlier did not clearly say otherwise. Can a family authorize a grief technology company to build a digital twin of a deceased relative who never had the chance to say yes or no to the idea while they were alive, because the technology to ask them did not yet exist. Each of these scenarios has already happened, in some form, somewhere, and the legal frameworks meant to answer them, discussed in detail in the chapters ahead on ownership and on the right to one's own face and voice, were mostly written for a world in which none of this was technically possible.

There is also a subtler version of the control question, one that has less to do with permission and more to do with fidelity. A digital twin is not a recording. It is a generative system, capable of producing new statements the original person never made. That means a digital twin can, in principle, keep changing after the person it represents has stopped changing, whether through retraining, through new data, or simply through the ordinary business decisions of whoever maintains it. A synthetic celebrity's opinions can be revised by committee. A deceased parent's digital twin can be updated with new conversational capabilities its creator never actually had. At what point does an AI representation stop being a faithful echo of a real person and start being something closer to a new character wearing that person's face and voice, shaped now by the incentives, however well-meaning, of whoever controls the system rather than by the person it was built to represent? Nobody has a clean answer to that question yet, including the companies building these systems, and it is likely to grow only more urgent as digital twins move from novelty to routine business and personal practice.

What synthetic celebrity and digital twins share, despite their very different origins, one built from nothing, the other built from someone, is that both are forcing a redefinition of identity that used to be settled by simple biological fact. A famous face used to belong, unambiguously, to the one person who had it. A voice used to be proof, on its own, that its owner had actually said the words attached to it. Neither assumption reliably holds anymore, and the chapters that follow spend considerable time on what should replace them: who owns the resulting creations, what rights a person retains over their own likeness once it can be convincingly separated from their living body, and how society might rebuild, deliberately this time, some of the trust that scarcity used to provide for free.

CHAPTER FOUR

Who Owns AI, and Who Owns What AI Creates

Of all the questions this book raises, the one most likely to end up decided in a courtroom rather than a philosophy seminar is this one: who owns an AI system, who owns the material used to build it, and who owns what it produces. Unlike questions of consciousness or personhood, which may never receive a final answer, ownership questions have to be answered, one way or another, because money is attached to them. A business cannot sell a product without knowing whether it actually has the right to sell it. A publisher cannot print a book without knowing whether the material inside it is legally protected. A court cannot resolve a dispute by shrugging.

It helps to separate what sounds like a single question into the several distinct questions it actually contains, because they do not all have the same answer, and treating them as one has caused a great deal of unnecessary confusion in public debate.

The Different Layers of Ownership

The first layer is ownership of the AI system itself: the software, the trained model, the infrastructure it runs on. This is the most straightforward layer, legally speaking, and works much like ownership of any other complex piece of software. Whoever built it, or whoever the builders assigned their rights to, generally owns it, protected through a mix of copyright in the code, trade secret protection over the exact training methods and internal weights, and sometimes patents on specific technical innovations.

The second layer is ownership, or at least the legal right to use, the data that trained the system. This layer has become the single most contested area of AI law in the years since large-scale generative models became commercially available, precisely because the models were trained on enormous quantities of text, images, and other material scraped from the internet, much of it created by people who never agreed to have their work used that way. Writers, visual artists, photographers, and news organizations have filed lawsuits across multiple countries arguing that training a commercial AI system on their copyrighted work without permission or payment is itself a form of infringement, regardless of what the system later generates. AI companies have generally argued that training a model on existing material is a transformative use, similar in principle to how a human artist learns by studying the work of others, and therefore does not require permission under exceptions like fair use in the United States. As of this writing, courts in multiple jurisdictions are still working through these arguments case by case, and the outcomes have been mixed enough that no single rule has emerged. This is, without exaggeration, one of the most consequential open legal questions of the decade, because its resolution will determine the basic economics of building AI systems at all.

The third layer, and the one this chapter spends the most time on, is ownership of what an AI system generates: the image, the song, the block of text, the synthetic voice recording, the digital persona built on top of all of them. This is where the law has actually started to produce concrete, citable answers, even while the first two layers remain unsettled, and those answers are worth understanding in detail because they will shape how every creator, business, and reader of this book can safely use these tools going forward.

The Fight Over Training Data

The second layer described above, the legal status of the material used to train an AI system, is worth pausing on longer, because it moved from abstract concern to concrete litigation faster than almost any other question in this book, and the outcome will shape the industry regardless of how the output-ownership questions discussed below are eventually resolved.

In December 2023, The New York Times filed suit against OpenAI and Microsoft, alleging that the companies had trained their AI systems on millions of the paper's copyrighted articles without permission or payment, and presenting evidence that the resulting systems could, in some cases, reproduce substantial portions of specific Times articles nearly verbatim when prompted in particular ways. The suit sought both damages and an order requiring the destruction of any AI models trained on the paper's copyrighted work, a remedy that, if granted, would have implications reaching far beyond a single newspaper. OpenAI and Microsoft disputed the claims, arguing that training an AI model on publicly available text is a transformative use protected by the fair use doctrine, comparable, in their framing, to a human researcher reading widely before forming their own original conclusions. As of this writing, the case remains in active litigation, and its eventual resolution is likely to become one of the single most consequential rulings in the history of American copyright law, precisely because nearly every major AI system was built using some version of the training approach being challenged.

A parallel set of cases has pursued the same underlying question from the perspective of visual artists rather than publishers. In Andersen v. Stability AI, filed in 2023, a group of artists sued the makers of several popular AI image generators, arguing that training the systems on billions of images scraped from the internet, including their own copyrighted artwork, without consent, constituted mass infringement, and that the resulting systems could be prompted to generate new images imitating a specific living artist's distinctive style closely enough to compete directly with that artist's own livelihood. Getty Images filed a related but separate suit against one of the same companies over the use of its licensed photography archive. Both cases have moved slowly through preliminary rulings that have narrowed and reshaped the specific claims at issue without yet resolving the central question either side actually cares about.

What all of these cases share, across two different creative industries and two different sets of plaintiffs, is a fight over whether the enormous economic value AI companies have built sits, at its foundation, on top of an enormous quantity of copyrighted material used without the consent or compensation ordinarily required to use someone else's protected work. Until that fight resolves, likely not in a single ruling but across a long sequence of cases in multiple courts and countries, every business built on top of a large AI model is operating with a real, unquantified legal exposure sitting somewhere upstream of its own product, inherited from decisions about training data made by a model provider the business itself had no part in and little visibility into.

What the Courts Have Actually Decided

Start with the United States, because its Copyright Office and courts have moved further than most on this specific question, and their reasoning has become an influential reference point even in countries with different legal traditions.

In September 2022, an artist named Kris Kashtanova received a copyright registration for a graphic novel titled Zarya of the Dawn, illustrated using the AI image generator Midjourney. The registration was granted before the Copyright Office realized how the images had been made. When the agency learned that the artwork was AI-generated, it reopened the registration and, in February 2023, issued a revised decision that has become a foundational reference point for how the office treats AI-assisted work. The Copyright Office drew a sharp line: the individual images, produced by typing descriptions into Midjourney and accepting what the tool generated, were not protected, because the actual expressive choices, the pixels, the composition of each individual picture, came from the machine's own process rather than from any direct human hand. But the graphic novel as a whole retained protection, because Kashtanova had made real, substantive creative decisions in selecting which images to use, arranging them into a sequence, combining them with original written text, and shaping the overall narrative. The output of the tool was not protectable. The human's creative arrangement of that output was.

That distinction, between the raw material a machine produces and the creative judgment a human applies in selecting, arranging, and building upon it, has held up as the closest thing to a working legal standard the United States currently has, and it echoes through nearly every subsequent decision on the subject.

The second major marker came from a very different kind of case. Stephen Thaler, a computer scientist, built an AI system he called the Creativity Machine and attempted to register copyright for an image it produced, listing the AI system itself as the sole author and Thaler as the owner by virtue of owning the machine. The Copyright Office refused, and Thaler sued. The case, Thaler v. Perlmutter, made its way to the United States Court of Appeals for the District of Columbia Circuit, which ruled against him in March 2025. The court's reasoning was, in its way, more sweeping than the Zarya decision, because it did not turn on how much creative judgment had been applied. It turned on a much simpler and more fundamental reading of the Copyright Act: the statute's language, its references to an author's lifespan, to inheritance by a widow or widower, to the requirement that rights be transferred by signature, presumes throughout that an author is a human being, capable of holding property, dying, and leaving heirs. A machine cannot do any of those things, the court held, and therefore cannot be an author under the statute as written, no matter how autonomously it generated the work in question. Crucially, the court was careful to note that this ruling did not touch the separate question of whether a human who uses AI as a tool, directing it, shaping it, exercising judgment over its output, can claim authorship over the resulting work. That question, the one Zarya of the Dawn had already begun to answer, remained open and, if anything, reinforced.

Read together, these two decisions sketch the shape of American copyright law's answer to artificial intelligence, at least for now: a machine cannot be an author, full stop, but a human who uses a machine as a sophisticated tool, the way a photographer uses a camera or a composer uses a synthesizer, can claim authorship over the results of that use, provided enough real human creative judgment shaped the outcome. The harder question, one the law has not yet settled with anything like the same clarity, is exactly how much human judgment is enough.

AI-Generated Versus AI-Assisted

That harder question is worth sitting with, because it is the one nearly every working creator, and every reader of this book who plans to use AI tools in their own work, actually needs an answer to.

Picture two people using the exact same AI image generator. The first types a single sentence, generates an image, and publishes the first result exactly as produced. The second starts with a rough sketch of their own, uses the AI tool to generate dozens of variations, rejects most of them, selects specific elements from several different outputs, combines them by hand in editing software, adjusts color and composition extensively, and repeats that cycle for hours before arriving at a final piece. Both people used the same underlying technology. The law, as it currently stands in the United States and in the reasoning UK courts have applied to their own, differently worded statute, is far more likely to recognize the second person's work as their own protected creation than the first person's, because the second process involved substantial, identifiable human authorship layered on top of the machine's raw output, while the first did not involve much more than clicking a button.

This is not a merely academic distinction. It has direct, practical consequences for anyone building a career, a business, or in the case of this book's own reader, a published work, around AI-assisted creation. A business that builds its entire product around AI-generated material with minimal human involvement may discover, too late, that it does not actually own the material it is selling, and cannot stop a competitor from using the identical AI tool to generate something functionally indistinguishable. A creator who documents their own process, keeping records of drafts, revisions, and the specific decisions they made along the way, is in a dramatically stronger position, both to claim copyright in the first place and to defend it later, than one who cannot show any meaningful trace of human judgment behind the finished work.

The United Kingdom has taken a notably different legislative path, worth understanding because it shows this is not a settled global consensus but an active, diverging experiment. Under Section 9(3) of the UK's Copyright, Designs and Patents Act 1988, a law written decades before anything resembling modern generative AI existed, a work generated by a computer with no human author is still eligible for copyright protection, and authorship is assigned to "the person by whom the arrangements necessary for the creation of the work are undertaken." In effect, the UK statute anticipated something like today's situation and built in an answer: rather than deny protection to fully machine-generated work the way the American approach does, it hands ownership to whoever set the process in motion, even if that person exercised comparatively little creative judgment over the specific result. The provision has existed for decades but has rarely been tested in court, and how it interacts with more recent, AI-specific developments remains genuinely unresolved, but it stands as a clear illustration that different legal systems, starting from different first principles, are answering the same underlying question in materially different ways. A creative work with no realistic claim to ownership in the United States might have a straightforward owner in the United Kingdom, and a global creative economy built on AI tools now has to account for that inconsistency directly rather than assuming one country's rule applies everywhere.

What This Means in Practice

Step back from the specific cases and a workable, practical principle emerges, one that is likely to remain useful even as the specific legal doctrines around it continue to evolve. Ownership, in the AI era, is tracking human creative contribution, not technical output. The camera did not make the photographer any less of an artist, because the choice of subject, framing, timing, and processing remained recognizably human. AI tools are following the same pattern, but the line demarking meaningful human contribution from a bare machine output is far blurrier with a text or image generator than it ever was with a camera, and that blurriness is exactly what courts, legislatures, and creators are all still working out in real time.

For any creator, business, or reader of this book planning to build something using AI tools, a few practical habits follow directly from everything above. Keep records of your actual process: drafts, prompts, revisions, and the specific choices you made along the way, because that record is what will distinguish your protectable creative work from an unprotectable machine output if the question is ever tested. Understand that different countries currently have different, sometimes contradictory rules, and that a global audience means potential exposure to more than one legal regime at once. And treat the current state of the law as a snapshot of an ongoing negotiation rather than a settled final answer, because the pace of litigation and legislation in this area has, if anything, accelerated rather than slowed as these tools have become more widely used.

The deeper question underneath all of this, one the next chapter takes up directly, is not really a legal question at all. It is a question about what creativity actually consists of, and what is genuinely left for a human being to contribute once a machine can generate the raw material of an image, a sentence, or a melody in a fraction of a second. The law is trying to answer that question because it has to. The rest of this book is trying to answer it because the answer matters for reasons that have nothing to do with courtrooms at all.

CHAPTER FIVE

The Human Contribution and the Future of Creativity

Every time a new technology has threatened to automate a creative act, the first response has been panic, and the second response, arriving a little later and with considerably less fanfare, has been a quiet redefinition of what the creative act actually was.

The clearest historical precedent is photography. When the camera arrived in the middle of the nineteenth century, it did something painters had spent centuries training to do by hand: it captured a scene exactly as it appeared, in far less time and with far more accuracy than the most skilled portraitist could manage. The French poet Charles Baudelaire, no technophobe by the standards of his era, wrote with real alarm about photography's threat to art, worried that a public seduced by mechanical exactness would lose its taste for anything requiring imagination or interpretation. He was not being unreasonable. A tool had just appeared that could do, instantly and mechanically, what painters had spent their entire careers learning to do by eye and by hand. If the value of painting was its ability to reproduce what a scene looked like, that value had just been undercut permanently.

Painting did not die. It changed what it was for. Within a few decades, a generation of painters that included the Impressionists deliberately abandoned photographic realism, not because they had lost the ability to paint representationally, but because representation was no longer the point. If a camera could capture what a haystack looked like at a single moment, a painter could instead spend a year capturing what the same haystack looked like under shifting light throughout an entire year, a project photography of that era could not easily replicate and that no camera could conceive of undertaking on its own. Painting moved from documentation toward interpretation, mood, and subjective vision, precisely because the documentary function had been taken over by a machine. The camera did not end visual art. It relocated the site of human contribution from execution to intention.

Something structurally similar is happening now with generative AI, across a far wider range of creative fields at once, and understanding the photography precedent helps clarify what is actually being automated and what is not.

A modern echo of that same argument played out in almost comic detail in April 2023, when a German artist named Boris Eldagsen won the creative open category of the Sony World Photography Awards, one of the most prestigious competitions in the field, for an eerie black-and-white portrait titled Pseudomnesia: The Electrician. Eldagsen then publicly declined the prize, revealing that the image had been generated entirely by AI and explaining that he had entered it deliberately, as an experiment, to test whether the competition's judges could tell the difference and to provoke a public conversation about where photography's boundaries actually lie. He was explicit that he had no interest in claiming the award under false pretenses, only in demonstrating, forcefully and publicly, that a competition built to honor photographic skill needed to reckon openly with images that involved no camera at all. The episode divided the photography world along lines that echo Baudelaire's nineteenth-century anxiety almost exactly, some arguing that Eldagsen had exposed a genuine crisis of definition the industry could no longer avoid, others arguing that the stunt proved nothing except that a sufficiently motivated person could generate a striking image and call it photography if a competition failed to ask the right question at the door. Both reactions were, in their way, correct, which is exactly why the episode is worth remembering: a field that had spent a century and a half absorbing the lesson painting learned from photography's arrival was now being asked to relearn a version of the same lesson itself, on a timeline of months rather than decades.

From Producer to Director

For most of the history of creative work, the ability to physically produce a finished piece, the brushstroke, the sentence, the chord progression, the line of code, was inseparable from the ability to conceive of it. A person who could not draw could not make a drawing, no matter how clear the image in their mind. A person who could not play an instrument could not record a melody they heard internally. Execution and conception were bottlenecked together, and most of the labor, and most of the training, that went into becoming a professional creator was labor spent closing the gap between what you could imagine and what your hands could actually produce.

Generative AI is prying those two things apart. A person with no drawing training can now direct an image generator through enough iterations to produce a specific visual result they had in mind. A person with no musical training can shape an AI composition tool toward a particular mood or structure through feedback and revision, even if they could not play a single note themselves. This does not eliminate skill from the process. It relocates it. The skill that used to live in your hand now needs to live in your judgment: your ability to recognize, out of a hundred generated options, which one is actually good, which one serves the piece, and which one is subtly wrong in a way that is easy to produce and hard to name.

This is a real skill, and it is not a lesser one simply because it looks different from the traditional craft skills it is displacing. Film directors have never needed to operate a camera, act every part, build every set, or compose the score themselves. Their skill has always been judgment, communicated through selection and direction rather than personal execution: knowing which take was the right take, which actor's interpretation served the scene, which of a composer's proposed themes actually belonged in the film. Generative AI is pushing a much wider range of creative work toward that directorial model. The musician working with AI-generated stems is choosing, arranging, and rejecting, the way a director chooses among takes. The novelist using an AI system to generate alternative phrasings for a difficult paragraph is exercising the same kind of editorial judgment an editor has always exercised over a writer's draft, just compressed into a single person's own process.

The uncomfortable implication, worth stating plainly, is that this shift rewards a different set of people than the old system did, and not always the people who spent years developing traditional craft skills. Someone with genuinely excellent taste and judgment, but historically little ability to execute that judgment by hand, is empowered by these tools in a way they never were before. Someone whose value came primarily from raw technical execution, the ability to render a photorealistic hand, to play a difficult passage flawlessly, to type quickly and cleanly, finds that specific value eroding, even if their underlying creative judgment is just as sound as it ever was. This is not a hypothetical tension. It is already reshaping hiring, commissioning, and compensation across illustration, music production, copywriting, and software development, and it is reasonable to expect it to keep doing so.

The Recording Academy, which administers the Grammy Awards, updated its eligibility rules in the years after generative AI music tools became widely available, drawing a line that closely tracks the distinction this book has already discussed in the context of copyright: a work that is entirely AI-generated, with no meaningful human authorship, is not eligible for consideration, while a work that uses AI tools as part of a genuinely human-directed creative process remains eligible, provided a human plays a meaningful creative role in writing or performing it. The Academy, in other words, arrived independently at essentially the same standard the Copyright Office had been developing: not whether AI touched the work, but how much authentic human judgment shaped the final result.

What Judgment Actually Requires

It is worth being specific about what this newly central skill, judgment, actually consists of, because "taste" can sound like an excuse for vague hand-waving rather than a real capacity that can be described and even, to some extent, developed deliberately.

Good creative judgment generally requires three things a generative AI system does not reliably have on its own. It requires a stable sense of purpose: knowing what a piece is actually for, who it needs to reach, and what it needs to accomplish for them, a context that usually sits outside the specific piece of content being generated and inside the messier situation the person commissioning it is trying to address. It requires the accumulated experience of having seen a great many attempts at similar work and having developed a feel, often difficult to articulate fully in words, for what tends to actually land with an audience versus what merely looks impressive in isolation. And it requires a willingness to say no, to reject a technically competent, even impressive, output because it is wrong for the specific purpose at hand, a judgment call that requires the discernment to notice the mismatch and the confidence to act on it rather than accepting whatever the tool most readily produces.

None of these three things are things an AI system currently supplies reliably on its own, because none of them are really about generating content. They are about knowing what should be generated in the first place, and why, a question that depends on context, stakes, and consequences the system itself has no access to and, on the technical description given in chapter one, no capacity to actually care about even if it did.

What Happens to the Apprenticeship

There is a structural risk in all of this that operates above the level of any single person's skill development, worth naming because it affects the pipeline that produces skilled judgment in the first place, not merely the individuals moving through it.

Nearly every field this book has touched has historically trained its most valuable judgment through an apprenticeship model, whether formally named that or not: a junior person spends years doing the more routine, more mechanical version of a craft, a paralegal drafting routine filings, a junior designer producing basic layout variations, a cub reporter covering minor local stories, under the supervision of someone more senior, and it is precisely that extended exposure to the routine version of the work that eventually produces the judgment needed to handle its harder, more consequential versions. The entry-level work is not merely a hurdle to clear on the way to a real career. It is the training data, to borrow a phrase from earlier chapters, that produces the senior judgment those same fields depend on a decade later.

Generative AI is disproportionately capable of automating precisely that entry-level, routine layer of work, the layer chapter two already identified as most exposed to disruption on economic grounds. The risk this raises is not only that junior workers lose a paycheck, serious as that is on its own. It is that the entire pipeline producing tomorrow's senior judgment quietly narrows, because the routine repetitions that used to build it are increasingly handled by a system rather than assigned to a person still learning the trade. A law firm that lets AI draft every routine filing saves real money in the short term and may, a decade later, discover it has no senior associates with the depth of practical experience the firm's more demanding work requires, because nobody spent the intervening years doing the unglamorous version of the job that used to build it.

No field has fully solved this problem yet, and it may require a genuinely new answer rather than simply preserving the old apprenticeship model by force. Some organizations have begun experimenting with deliberately preserving unassisted, supervised practice for their most junior staff even where AI tools could technically do the same work faster, treating that practice explicitly as a training investment rather than a production inefficiency to be optimized away. Whether that approach scales, or whether an entirely different model for building senior-level judgment eventually replaces the apprenticeship system altogether, is one of the more consequential open questions this book raises without being able to resolve.

The Authenticity Premium

One economic pattern is already visible enough to name with some confidence, and it runs in the opposite direction from what a purely efficiency-driven reading of AI's rise might predict: as machine-produced content becomes abundant and nearly free, a meaningful segment of the market has started paying a real premium for things explicitly marketed as unassisted human work.

This is not a new pattern invented in response to AI. It has a well-documented precedent in the music industry's relationship with vinyl records, a format that all but disappeared commercially once compact discs and, later, digital streaming offered obviously superior convenience and audio consistency. Vinyl did not stay dead. It has spent the past two decades in sustained commercial revival, driven largely by listeners willing to pay significantly more for a physically inferior, less convenient format precisely because of the qualities digital perfection cannot offer: the audible imperfection of analog sound, the physical ritual of handling a record, the sense of a tangible object with a history rather than an infinitely reproducible file. Digital abundance did not eliminate demand for the analog alternative. It created the conditions for that alternative to become a deliberate, premium choice rather than simply the default.

Something similar is already emerging around AI-generated content. Labels reading "human-written," "no AI," or "handmade" have begun appearing on everything from freelance writing marketplaces to artisanal goods to news publications explicitly marketing their reporting as untouched by generative tools, aimed at a segment of consumers for whom the knowledge of unassisted human effort is itself part of what they are paying for, not merely a byproduct of the purchase. Whether this authenticity premium remains a durable niche market or grows into something closer to a mainstream expectation remains genuinely uncertain, and probably depends heavily on how the trust and provenance questions explored in the next chapter get resolved. What seems reasonably safe to predict is that it will not disappear. The value of a thing partly reflects its scarcity, and once machine-generated content becomes the abundant default in a given category, demonstrable human effort becomes, by the same logic that has always governed scarcity and value, more valuable rather than less.

A Note of Caution

None of this should curdle into complacency, because there is a real risk sitting alongside the real opportunity, and a book that only described the opportunity would be doing its reader a disservice.

The concern is not that AI will replace human judgment outright. It is that easy access to competent-looking AI output will quietly erode the conditions under which good judgment actually develops in the first place. Judgment of the kind described above is not innate. It is built, gradually, through the accumulated experience of trying things, getting them wrong, and developing an internal sense of quality through direct contact with the difficulty of the work. A young writer develops an ear for a good sentence partly by writing a great many bad ones first. A young designer develops an eye for composition partly by producing a great many compositions that do not quite work and slowly learning why. If AI tools make it possible to skip straight to competent-looking output without ever passing through that difficult, occasionally humbling process of producing something bad and learning from exactly how it is bad, an entire generation of creators risks arriving at the judgment stage of their careers without ever having built the underlying instincts that judgment depends on.

This concern has a real precedent, and it is worth taking seriously rather than dismissing as generational nostalgia. Calculators did not eliminate the value of mathematical reasoning, but educators have spent decades arguing about how much basic arithmetic fluency students need before they are allowed to reach for a calculator, precisely because a certain kind of numerical intuition seems to depend on having done the work by hand at some point. GPS navigation has measurably eroded some people's ability to independently navigate unfamiliar places, a finding replicated across multiple studies of spatial cognition. There is no reason to assume creative judgment is somehow immune to a similar erosion if the harder, slower parts of the creative process are bypassed too early and too completely.

The responsible position, for an individual creator, a parent, an educator, or a business making decisions about how deeply to integrate these tools, is not to avoid AI-assisted creation, which would forfeit real and legitimate benefits, but to remain deliberate about preserving the harder, slower experiences that actually build judgment in the first place, even when a faster path is available. That might mean a writing program that still requires a first year of unassisted drafting before AI tools are introduced. It might mean a design studio that still runs internal exercises with no AI involved at all, purely to keep its junior staff's independent eye sharp. The specific practices will vary by field. The underlying principle will not: judgment is downstream of struggle, and a technology that removes all the struggle risks, over time, removing the judgment it was supposed to serve.

The chapters ahead turn from the question of what humans contribute to creative work toward an equally pressing question: how anyone, creator or audience, is supposed to tell what is real in the first place, once the tools for producing convincing fabrication have become as accessible as the tools for producing anything else.

CHAPTER SIX

Watermarks, Provenance, and the Death of Easy Authenticity

For most of modern history, seeing and hearing have functioned as a kind of proof. A photograph documented that something had happened in front of a lens. A recording captured a voice actually speaking actual words. A video showed an event unfolding in a specific place at a specific time. None of these media were perfectly reliable, and people who worked closely with them always knew it, but for the ordinary person going about an ordinary day, the rule of thumb held well enough to be trustworthy: if you could see it or hear it clearly, it probably happened.

That rule of thumb no longer holds the way it used to, not because people have suddenly become more deceptive, but because fabrication convincing enough to fool a careful viewer no longer requires real skill, real time, or real equipment, only a laptop and a piece of software available to anyone. A face can be generated that never belonged to any real person. A voice can be cloned convincingly enough to fool a family member on the phone. A video can show a real public figure saying something they never said, with lip movements, tone, and timing that survive a casual viewing without any visible seam. The question this raises is not new in kind, only in scale and accessibility: how do we know what is real?

Authenticity Crises Are Not New

It helps, before turning to the current moment, to remember that the anxiety about manufactured reality is one of the oldest anxieties in the history of images, not a brand-new problem invented by artificial intelligence.

Art forgery has existed for as long as art has had market value, and some forgers achieved a level of skill that fooled the most credentialed experts of their era for years at a time. The Dutch forger Han van Meegeren spent the 1930s and 1940s producing fake paintings in the style of Johannes Vermeer, good enough that respected art historians authenticated them as genuine seventeenth-century masterpieces. Van Meegeren sold one of his fakes to Hermann Göring during the Nazi occupation of the Netherlands, and after the war he was arrested for collaboration, accused of selling an irreplaceable Dutch national treasure to a senior Nazi official. His defense was almost too strange to believe: he insisted the painting was not a genuine Vermeer at all but his own forgery, meaning he was guilty of fraud rather than treason. Prosecutors did not believe him, so van Meegeren proved it the only way he could, by painting an entirely new fake Vermeer from scratch in front of court-appointed witnesses while under arrest. It worked. He was convicted of forgery instead of collaboration, a considerably lesser charge, and the episode remains one of the most vivid demonstrations in history that expert human judgment, applied confidently and in good faith, can be wrong about authenticity for a very long time.

Photography, the very medium whose credibility artificial intelligence is now undermining, was never as purely truthful as its reputation suggested. Official photographs of Soviet leadership were routinely retouched to remove officials who had fallen out of favor or been executed, erasing them from the historical visual record as thoroughly as if they had never stood in the frame at all. Composite photography, combining multiple negatives into a single deceptive image, was common practice within a few decades of photography's invention, and the Victorian era produced an entire minor industry of faked spirit photographs, purporting to show ghostly apparitions of the dead standing behind grieving family members. In 1917, two young cousins in England produced a series of photographs that appeared to show them alongside genuine fairies. The images were crude paper cutouts photographed at a deceptive angle, and they nonetheless convinced a number of credulous adults for years, including, most famously, Sir Arthur Conan Doyle, the creator of Sherlock Holmes, a man whose fictional detective was built entirely around the discipline of skeptical, evidence-based reasoning.

The point of this brief history is not that artificial intelligence poses no new problem. It plainly does. The point is that the underlying vulnerability, human willingness to trust a convincing image or a convincing voice more readily than the situation warrants, is not a new weakness that AI has discovered. It is a very old weakness that AI has simply made dramatically cheaper and faster to exploit, at a scale no individual forger working alone could ever have approached.

The Deepfake Present

That difference in scale and accessibility is not an abstraction. It has already produced real, documented harm, in contexts far more consequential than an art market or a Victorian parlor trick.

On the eve of New Hampshire's presidential primary in January 2024, thousands of Democratic voters received a robocall carrying an AI-generated voice closely imitating President Biden, urging them to stay home rather than vote in the primary. The call was traced to a political consultant named Steve Kramer, who later claimed he had orchestrated it as a demonstration of AI's dangers rather than a genuine attempt at voter suppression, a defense that did not spare him from being indicted on felony voter suppression charges or from a proposed six million dollar fine from the Federal Communications Commission. The episode became a template that election officials and technology companies have referenced repeatedly since: a synthetic voice, built from widely available public recordings of a well-known figure's speech, deployed at essentially zero marginal cost to reach thousands of people simultaneously, with a message designed to interfere with a basic democratic process. Nothing about the technology involved was exotic or difficult to obtain. That was precisely the point, and precisely the danger.

Music offered an earlier and, in its way, more culturally revealing preview of the same underlying problem. In early 2023, a track called "Heart on My Sleeve" appeared online featuring what sounded unmistakably like the voices of the musicians Drake and The Weeknd, performing a song neither of them had actually recorded. It had been produced entirely with AI voice-cloning tools by an anonymous creator, and it spread widely enough, drawing millions of streams before it was pulled from major platforms, that the Recording Academy felt compelled to publicly clarify it would not be eligible for Grammy consideration regardless of its popularity, because no genuine human performance by the credited artists existed behind it. The episode was treated by much of the press as a curiosity, a viral novelty rather than a serious problem, but it demonstrated something that should have been sobering rather than amusing: a convincing simulation of two of the most recognizable voices in contemporary music, created without either artist's knowledge or consent, could reach a mass audience and be widely mistaken for the real thing before anyone with the authority to stop it had a chance to intervene.

These are the headline-grabbing cases. A much larger and quieter harm has accumulated in parallel, affecting private individuals rather than presidents and pop stars: non-consensual synthetic imagery used to harass, intimidate, or extort ordinary people, overwhelmingly women, who never sought any public attention at all and now have to contend with fabricated content bearing their face circulating beyond their control. This dimension of the problem receives fuller treatment in the next chapter, on the right to one's own face and voice, but it belongs in any honest accounting of what has already gone wrong, not only what might go wrong someday.

When Newsrooms Got Ahead of Themselves

Not every authenticity failure involves a deliberate deception, and it is worth including at least one example of good-faith institutional overreach alongside the deliberate fraud described above, because the lesson it offers is different and, for most organizations weighing whether to adopt these tools, considerably more relevant.

In January 2023, the technology news outlet CNET revealed, after being asked directly by an outside reporter who had noticed something odd about the tone of certain articles, that it had quietly been publishing dozens of finance explainer articles written by an AI system, under a byline that identified only as "CNET Money Staff" rather than disclosing the AI involvement clearly. Once the practice came to light, CNET undertook its own internal review and found that more than half of the AI-generated articles it examined contained factual errors significant enough to require correction, some of them fundamental mistakes about how compound interest or loan terms actually worked, the kind of error a competent human financial writer would have been unlikely to make and unlikely to have gone through several rounds of professional editing without catching. CNET paused the practice, issued corrections, and stated it would resume using AI-assisted writing only with clearer disclosure and stronger human editorial review built into the process.

Nothing about the CNET episode involved bad intent in the way the New Hampshire robocall or the fabricated Drake and The Weeknd track did. It involved a reputable organization moving faster than its own verification processes could support, trusting a fluent, confident-sounding output without building the review infrastructure that fluency alone does not make unnecessary. That distinction matters for how this book's argument applies beyond the clearest cases of fraud, and it echoes a warning from chapter one worth restating directly here: a system trained to produce statistically plausible text will produce output that reads as authoritative regardless of whether it is accurate, and an organization's own credibility offers no special protection against publishing confident nonsense if it skips the human verification step that credibility was always actually built on.

Building an Infrastructure of Trust

The response taking shape across the technology industry, governments, and journalism is not a single tool but an entire emerging infrastructure, and it is worth understanding in outline because some version of it will likely become as ordinary, and as invisible, as the padlock icon in a web browser.

The most developed effort is a technical standard called C2PA, the Coalition for Content Provenance and Authenticity, formed in 2021 by a partnership that has grown to include Adobe, Microsoft, the BBC, Intel, and a long and expanding list of other technology and media organizations. The underlying idea is straightforward even though the engineering behind it is not: attach a secure, cryptographically verifiable record to a piece of media at the moment of its creation, documenting what device or software produced it, whether AI was involved, and what edits were subsequently made to it, all the way through its distribution. A photograph carrying this kind of credential would let a viewer, or more realistically the platform hosting it, trace its history back to the camera that captured it, rather than simply trusting that it looks plausible. The same infrastructure can flag, rather than trying to hide, the fact that a given image or video involved AI generation at some stage of its life.

Regulation has begun moving in a similar direction. The European Union's AI Act, which entered into force in August 2024, includes transparency obligations requiring that certain categories of AI-generated content, including deepfakes and AI systems interacting directly with the public, be clearly disclosed as artificial rather than presented as unmediated human output. Other jurisdictions have moved more narrowly and more quickly on specific harms, several American states passing laws specifically targeting election-related deepfakes and non-consensual synthetic imagery in the wake of cases like the New Hampshire robocall, without waiting for a comprehensive federal framework that has, as of this writing, not yet arrived.

None of this infrastructure is close to complete, and none of it should be mistaken for a finished solution. It represents the early stage of a much longer institutional effort, roughly comparable to where digital security stood in the early days of encryption for online banking: a real technical foundation, increasingly adopted by major players, still years away from being so ubiquitous that ordinary users stop noticing it is there at all.

The Limits of Verification

Even a fully mature version of this infrastructure would not solve the underlying problem completely, and it is worth being honest about why, rather than presenting provenance technology as a clean fix.

A watermark or a piece of provenance metadata can be stripped, deliberately or accidentally, at almost any point in a piece of content's journey across the internet. A screenshot of a video defeats most embedded metadata instantly, because the screenshot is a new file with no inherited history of its own. A sufficiently motivated bad actor, willing to route around whichever platforms enforce provenance standards most strictly, can usually find some path to an audience that does not check. And the C2PA standard itself makes no claim to solve the deeper problem at all: it documents where a piece of content came from and what has been done to it, but it explicitly does not, and cannot, certify that the content is true, accurate, or fair. A real photograph, taken by a real camera with full, verifiable provenance, can still be staged, selectively cropped, or presented with a deliberately misleading caption. Provenance tells you where something came from. It does not tell you what it means, and conflating the two is its own kind of mistake.

What this suggests is that the coming decades will likely require a shift in what authenticity itself is understood to mean, away from a purely perceptual test, does this look and sound real, and toward something closer to an institutional and procedural test, can this be verified through a traceable chain of custody, and do I trust the institutions maintaining that chain. This is, in fact, closer to how a great deal of modern life already works than people tend to notice. Almost nobody personally verifies that a bill of currency is not counterfeit by examining its physical properties; they trust a system of institutions, security features, and legal consequences that makes counterfeiting difficult and rare enough to make casual trust reasonable. Almost nobody personally verifies a news article's underlying reporting; they trust, to varying and often justified degrees, the editorial and fact-checking processes of the publication behind it. The verification of synthetic media is likely to develop along a similar path: not a world in which every individual has personally developed the forensic skill to detect an AI-generated video, which is already becoming an unrealistic expectation for most people, but a world in which trust gets outsourced to platforms, standards, and institutions that have done the harder verification work upstream, the same way trust in currency and journalism already works today.

That shift will not be comfortable, and it will not arrive quickly or evenly. It will also not be optional. The alternative, a public that has simply stopped trusting anything it sees or hears because it has become too difficult to tell the difference, is arguably the more dangerous outcome of the two, corrosive not just to any specific piece of content but to the shared factual ground that public discourse, elections, journalism, and ordinary trust between people all depend on. Building the infrastructure described in this chapter, imperfect and unfinished as it currently is, is not a minor technical footnote to the AI story. It may turn out to be one of the more consequential institutional projects of the next decade, because so much else depends on getting it right.

Labeling Is Not Neutral

The regulatory response described above, requiring disclosure when content is AI-generated, sounds, at first pass, like an uncontroversial solution: simply require a label, and let audiences decide for themselves how much weight to give the content accordingly. China moved fastest and most comprehensively on exactly this approach. Rules issued by the Cyberspace Administration of China, building on measures first proposed in 2023, require platforms operating in the country to clearly label AI-generated text, images, audio, and video, and require creators to disclose when they are posting synthetic content, backed by real enforcement authority against platforms that fail to comply. It is, on paper, one of the most comprehensive labeling regimes in the world.

But labeling turns out to raise its own difficult questions rather than simply resolving the authenticity problem cleanly. A political cartoon, a piece of satire, or a work of speculative fiction has always been understood by its audience as something other than a literal factual claim, without needing an explicit label to establish that shared understanding. Requiring the same explicit disclosure for a clearly satirical AI-generated image that a reasonable audience would never mistake for documentary fact risks treating parody and fraud as the same category of problem, when they plainly are not, and some free expression advocates have raised exactly this concern about broad, undifferentiated labeling mandates. There is also a harder practical problem sitting underneath the policy question: a labeling regime only works if it is actually followed, and the same accessibility that makes AI content generation available to a well-intentioned educator or artist makes it equally available to someone with no interest whatsoever in complying with a disclosure law, particularly when they can route around whichever platform is enforcing it and toward one that is not, or is operating from outside the regulating country's jurisdiction entirely.

None of this is an argument against labeling requirements, which remain, on balance, a reasonable and probably necessary piece of the trust infrastructure described in this chapter. It is a reminder that no single policy tool, however sensible, fully closes the gap this chapter has been describing. Labeling helps audiences who see the label. It does nothing for audiences who encounter the same content stripped of it, willfully or otherwise, which is precisely why the deeper, harder work of building verifiable provenance, rather than relying on disclosure alone, remains necessary alongside it rather than instead of it.

The next chapter turns from authenticity in general to something more personal and, for many readers, more urgent: what happens to your own face, your own voice, and your own name once the tools to convincingly reproduce all three are only a few clicks away from anyone who wants to use them, with or without your permission.

CHAPTER SEVEN

The Right to Your Face, Voice, and Digital Self

Your face is recognizable. Your voice is recognizable. Your name is recognizable, and if you have spent any real time in public life, your mannerisms, your turns of phrase, and your general manner probably are too. Until recently, none of that recognizability required much legal protection, because reproducing it convincingly took real skill, real resources, or a real relationship with you. An impersonator needed genuine talent. A ghostwriter needed your actual cooperation. A photograph needed an actual camera pointed at your actual face. The difficulty of imitation was, itself, a kind of protection, one that never had to be written into law because it was built into the physical and economic cost of faking anything convincingly.

That built-in protection is gone. What follows is the story of how the law has tried, in fits and starts, spread across more than a century, to build a replacement for it, and how badly that replacement is currently straining against a technology that can now clone a voice from eleven seconds of audio and generate a photorealistic face that never belonged to anyone at all.

A Right Built From Nothing

The right of publicity, the legal principle that gives a person some control over the commercial use of their own name, image, and likeness, has a surprisingly short and specific history for something so fundamental to how public figures now manage their careers. Its intellectual roots trace back to an 1890 law review article by Samuel Warren and Louis Brandeis, later a Supreme Court justice, arguing that American law needed to recognize a general "right to privacy" that earlier legal traditions had never clearly established, largely in response to intrusive newspaper photography and gossip reporting of their era. That article shaped privacy law for decades, but it was not until 1953, in a dispute over baseball trading cards, that an American court first articulated something closer to what we now call the right of publicity as distinct from privacy: the idea that a person, particularly a famous one, has a property interest in the commercial value of their own identity, separate from any claim about emotional distress or reputational harm. A company that used a baseball player's photograph on a trading card without permission was not just invading his privacy, the court reasoned. It was taking something of clear commercial value that belonged to him.

From that starting point, the right of publicity grew unevenly, state by state, into the patchwork that still exists today. The United States has never adopted a single federal right of publicity. Instead, each state has developed its own version, some through legislation, some purely through court decisions, with meaningfully different rules about what counts as a violation, how long the right lasts after death, and how it interacts with free speech protections. California and New York, homes to the entertainment industry, developed particularly robust versions. Other states offer far thinner protection. A public figure's legal recourse against having their identity exploited without consent can therefore depend, in a way that feels almost arbitrary, on which state's law happens to apply to the dispute.

Tennessee's version of this law has an origin story that connects directly to this book's opening chapters. After Elvis Presley died in 1977, his estate fought a series of legal battles over who had the right to control the commercial use of his name and image, disputes significant enough that Tennessee passed the Personal Rights Protection Act of 1984 largely in response, explicitly extending publicity rights to continue after a person's death rather than ending at the moment they die. Four decades later, that same legislative lineage produced the ELVIS Act, discussed at more length below, when Tennessee lawmakers looked at what AI voice cloning was doing to their state's enormous music industry and decided the 1984 law needed an update built specifically for the moment when a voice, not just a name or a photograph, could be stolen wholesale.

Sound-Alikes and the Limits of Imitation

Long before AI made voice cloning cheap and precise, the law had already been forced to confront a related question: what happens when someone does not use your actual voice at all, but hires someone else to imitate it closely enough that audiences assume it is you?

In 1988, the singer Bette Midler sued the Ford Motor Company after Ford's advertising agency, having been turned down by Midler herself for a car commercial, hired one of Midler's own former backup singers and specifically instructed her to imitate Midler's distinctive vocal style as closely as possible. No recording of Midler's actual voice was used anywhere in the commercial. Every element of it was, technically, someone else's original performance. The United States Court of Appeals for the Ninth Circuit ruled in Midler's favor anyway, in a decision that has shaped celebrity voice rights ever since. A voice, the court held, can be so closely identified with a particular person that deliberately imitating it for commercial purposes, in order to capitalize on the audience's association with that specific individual, violates that person's right of publicity even without using a single second of their actual recorded voice. A few years later, a similar case brought by the musician Tom Waits against Frito-Lay reinforced the same principle. The law, in other words, had already recognized decades before generative AI existed that a voice deserves protection as an element of identity in its own right, not merely as a physical recording that can be copied or not copied.

That precedent matters enormously for the AI era, because it suggests courts already have a workable legal theory for a problem that might otherwise seem to require entirely new law: a synthetic voice trained to evoke a specific real person, even if it is technically a new, AI-generated performance rather than a direct copy of any single recording, can plausibly be treated the same way the law has treated human sound-alikes for decades. The remaining question is not whether the underlying legal principle exists. It clearly does. The question is whether it can be enforced quickly and affordably enough to matter against a technology that can produce an infringing voice clone in minutes, for a cost approaching zero, from anywhere in the world.

The ELVIS Act

Tennessee answered that question directly in 2024. Governor Bill Lee signed the Ensuring Likeness, Voice, and Image Security Act, universally known by its acronym, into law on March 21 of that year, after the bill passed both chambers of the Tennessee legislature without a single dissenting vote, ninety-three to nothing in the House and thirty to nothing in the Senate. The unanimous margin reflected the extraordinary alignment behind it: Nashville's music industry, songwriters, performers, and recording studios alike, treated unauthorized AI voice cloning as an existential threat to a business built almost entirely on the commercial value of distinctive human voices, and lobbied hard for a fix.

The ELVIS Act works by amending Tennessee's existing 1984 publicity rights law to explicitly add voice to the list of protected attributes alongside name, photograph, and likeness, and by adding specific provisions aimed squarely at AI. It makes the unauthorized use of AI to replicate a person's voice a Class A misdemeanor and creates civil liability for anyone who distributes technology whose primary purpose is producing unauthorized vocal or likeness replicas of a specific person. It was, by a meaningful margin, the first law in the United States written with generative AI voice cloning specifically in mind, rather than adapted after the fact from older statutes built for a different kind of threat, and it has since become a reference model other states have looked to as they draft their own versions.

The Scarlett Johansson Episode

A few weeks after the ELVIS Act took effect, an entirely different kind of controversy illustrated exactly why lawmakers had felt such urgency. In May 2024, OpenAI unveiled a new conversational voice for its ChatGPT product named Sky, warm, slightly breathy, and strikingly reminiscent, to a great many listeners, of the actress Scarlett Johansson, who had voiced an AI character in the 2013 film Her, a movie explicitly referenced during OpenAI's own product demonstration.

Johansson stated publicly that OpenAI's chief executive had approached her twice, asking her to license her actual voice for the product, and that she had declined both times, citing personal reasons. When the Sky voice launched sounding, to her and to many others, close enough to her own voice to cause confusion, she said she was "shocked, angered, and in disbelief" and retained legal counsel. OpenAI paused the Sky voice within days, stated that it had never intended to imitate Johansson and that the voice belonged to a different, independently hired actress, and maintained that the resemblance was coincidental. The dispute was never fully litigated in court, so no judge ever ruled on whose account was legally correct. What the episode demonstrated regardless of its unresolved outcome was the practical gap this chapter has been describing: even one of the most well-resourced AI companies in the world, fully aware of the legal risk after having been directly asked and directly declined, still shipped a product that a global audience, and the person it allegedly resembled, immediately perceived as an appropriation of a specific, recognizable identity. If a sophisticated company operating under intense public scrutiny can stumble into that outcome, the risk facing an ordinary person with no legal team and no public platform is considerably harder to manage, not easier.

Performers as a Class

The Screen Actors Guild-American Federation of Television and Radio Artists, the primary American union representing film, television, and audio performers, made artificial intelligence the central issue of its historic 2023 strike, alongside more familiar disputes over streaming residuals. The union's specific concern went beyond any single celebrity's individual voice. It centered on background performers and stunt actors, workers routinely scanned for a single day's digital double work under contracts that, before the strike, often granted broad and effectively permanent rights to reuse that digital scan indefinitely, in projects the original performer might never even be told about, without any additional consent or compensation beyond the original day's pay.

The agreement that ended the strike established, for the first time in the American entertainment industry, contractual requirements for informed consent and specific compensation before a performer's digital replica could be used, along with restrictions on training AI systems on a performer's voice or likeness without their union representation's involvement. It did not resolve every open question, and disputes over exactly how the new provisions apply in practice have continued since, but it represented the first time an entire major American labor union had successfully negotiated enforceable, industry-wide protections specifically against unauthorized AI replication of its members' identities, a template other unions and other countries have since studied closely.

Beyond Celebrities

It would be a mistake to treat any of this as primarily a celebrity problem, even though celebrities generate the headlines. Ordinary people face a version of the same exposure, often with far fewer resources to fight back.

Illinois offers the most instructive example of what protection for ordinary people can look like when it exists. The state's Biometric Information Privacy Act, passed in 2008, long before anyone was worrying about generative AI, requires companies to obtain informed written consent before collecting a person's biometric identifiers, a category that includes face and voice prints, and critically, unlike similar laws in most other states, allows individual citizens to sue over violations directly rather than relying entirely on a state regulator to act on their behalf. That private right of action turned out to matter enormously once large technology companies began building facial recognition and biometric features into consumer products at scale. Facebook, now Meta, agreed to pay $650 million in 2021 to settle a class action brought under the law over its photo-tagging facial recognition feature, one of the largest privacy settlements in American history at the time, and the same statute has since been used against numerous other companies collecting biometric data without proper consent. Most states have no equivalent law, meaning a resident of Illinois currently has meaningfully stronger legal standing to challenge unauthorized use of their own biometric data, including their face, than a resident of almost anywhere else in the country.

The most severe version of unauthorized identity replication involves non-consensual sexually explicit deepfake imagery, disproportionately targeting women and, with increasing frequency, minors, generated using ordinary photographs scraped from social media and readily available AI tools that require no special expertise to operate. This is not a marginal problem confined to obscure corners of the internet; it has affected public figures and private individuals alike, including documented cases involving public school students creating explicit deepfakes of their own classmates. A federal bill called the DEFIANCE Act, which would give victims of this specific harm a civil cause of action, the right to sue for damages against people who create or knowingly distribute non-consensual intimate imagery generated or manipulated using AI, has passed the Senate by unanimous vote twice, first in 2024 and again in early

2026, only to stall both times in the House of Representatives without reaching a president's desk. Victims are left, in the meantime, dependent on the uneven patchwork of state laws described throughout this chapter, since no federal civil remedy for this specific harm currently exists despite two separate rounds of unanimous Senate support. Even fully enacted, such a law would only address the harm after it occurs. It would do nothing to prevent the underlying tools from being used this way in the first place, a gap no law anywhere has yet managed to close.

A Different Legal Tradition

Everything described so far in this chapter reflects a distinctly American legal approach, built case by case around the specific concept of a right of publicity. It is worth noting, briefly, that other legal traditions have reached for a different set of tools to protect much the same underlying interest, because the contrast clarifies what is actually at stake.

The European Union's General Data Protection Regulation, which took effect in 2018, does not use the language of publicity rights at all. It instead treats a person's biometric data, including facial geometry and voice characteristics, as a special category of personal data requiring explicit, informed consent before collection or use, backed by some of the most consequential privacy enforcement powers in the world. That enforcement power was demonstrated directly in the context of AI itself when Italy's data protection authority temporarily suspended ChatGPT's availability in the country in March 2023, citing concerns about the lawful basis for OpenAI's data processing, before lifting the suspension roughly a month later once the company made specific changes to its disclosures and user controls. Italy's regulator returned to the issue in December 2024, fining OpenAI fifteen million euros over how the company had handled personal data before those changes were made. Where the American approach protects a person's identity primarily as a form of commercial property, something that can be licensed, sold, and litigated over as an economic asset, the European approach protects it primarily as a matter of personal dignity and data control, a right that exists independent of whether any commercial use or financial harm is involved at all. A public figure's voice, under the European framework, does not need to have commercial value for its unauthorized collection and use to raise a legal problem; the mere processing of that biometric data without proper legal basis is enough.

This divergence matters practically, not just academically, for exactly the reason chapter four raised in the different context of copyright: a global AI industry now has to build products that satisfy two, and often more, structurally different legal philosophies at once, and a practice that is merely risky in one jurisdiction can be a serious, actively enforced violation in another. Any company, or any individual reader of this book building a product around synthetic voices or faces, needs to understand which tradition, or which combination of traditions, actually governs the market they intend to operate in, because assuming American rules apply everywhere, or that European rules are simply a stricter version of the same thing, has already proven to be an expensive mistake for more than one company operating in this space.

Toward a Right to the Digital Self

Taken together, the ELVIS Act, the Midler precedent, the Johansson episode, the SAG-AFTRA agreement, Illinois's biometric privacy law, and the stalled federal effort behind the DEFIANCE Act do not yet add up to a single, coherent legal framework. They are closer to early, disconnected repairs to a structure that was never built to withstand this particular kind of pressure, each one responding to whichever specific harm became visible and politically urgent enough to act on first.

A more complete answer, one that legal scholars and advocacy groups have already begun sketching even if no jurisdiction has fully enacted it, would likely need to establish a few consistent principles across every state and, ideally, every country: that a person's face, voice, and likeness belong to them by default, requiring affirmative consent before commercial or public use rather than requiring the person to discover and object after the fact. That consent should be specific rather than blanket, covering a particular use rather than signing away control indefinitely through fine print nobody reads. That compensation should follow whenever someone else profits from a person's likeness, in rough proportion to the value it generates for them. That rights should survive a person's death for some defined period, protecting family and legacy, without extending forever in a way that freezes a public figure's identity out of legitimate historical or creative use by later generations. And that enforcement needs to be fast and accessible enough to matter against a technology that can produce a violation in minutes, because a right that takes years of expensive litigation to vindicate is, for most people, barely a right at all.

None of this is fully in place anywhere yet. All of it is being actively fought over, state by state and case by case, right now, while you read this chapter. The next chapter turns to a different, in some ways more intimate question raised by the same underlying technology: not who controls a synthetic face or voice, but what it means for a real human being to form a genuine emotional attachment to one.

CHAPTER EIGHT

AI Companions, Synthetic Relationships, and Human Connection

Of every artificial identity described in this book, the ones most likely to matter most intimately to an individual reader are not the celebrities, the employees, or the digital twins of the famous dead. They are the quiet ones: the AI companion someone opens every night before falling asleep, the character someone has been talking to for two years and has come to think of, whatever the label technically means, as a friend.

This chapter takes that category seriously, on its own terms, rather than treating it as a punchline or a cautionary tale dressed up as analysis. Millions of people already use AI companions regularly. Dismissing the phenomenon as sad or pathetic tells us nothing useful about why it is happening at such scale, and offers no help at all to the people, likely including someone you know personally, already in the middle of it.

The Loneliness Backdrop

AI companionship did not create the need it is meeting. It arrived into a society that had already been measuring, with real alarm, a documented decline in the kind of ordinary social connection people have historically relied on. In May 2023, the United States Surgeon General, Vivek Murthy, released a formal advisory describing loneliness and isolation as a public health epidemic, citing evidence that chronic loneliness carries mortality risk comparable to smoking up to fifteen cigarettes a day and is associated with significantly elevated risk of heart disease, dementia, and premature death. The advisory pointed to measurable declines in time spent with friends, participation in community organizations, and the size of people's close social networks, trends that predated AI companion apps by years and that the advisory attributed to a broad mix of causes: work patterns, suburban design, the decline of religious and civic participation, and the attention-capturing pull of existing digital media.

An AI companion did not cause that underlying isolation. It arrived as one of the first widely available products explicitly designed to address it directly, on demand, at three in the morning, for the price of a monthly subscription. Understanding AI companionship without understanding the loneliness it is responding to is like trying to understand why people buy umbrellas without acknowledging that it is raining.

How These Bonds Actually Form

Replika, one of the earliest and most widely used AI companion apps, has an origin story worth knowing because it captures, in miniature, exactly why this category of product resonates so strongly. Its creator, Eugenia Kuyda, lost a close friend, Roman Mazurenko, in a car accident in 2015. Grieving, she gathered his old text messages and fed them into a simple neural network, producing a chatbot that could respond in something like his patterns of speech. She found comfort in being able to revisit those patterns in an interactive form rather than as a static archive of old messages, and the experience of building that private memorial led her to build Replika as a general product, launched publicly in November 2017. It grew from two million users within its first year to more than thirty million within seven years, evidence of an appetite that clearly went well beyond a small niche of technology enthusiasts.

The psychological mechanism behind that growth is not mysterious, and this book has already introduced its earliest documented example. Chapter one described Joseph Weizenbaum's 1966 chatbot ELIZA, and his startled discovery that people confided in it as though it understood them, despite knowing, explicitly, that it did not. An AI companion available today does everything ELIZA did and a great deal more: it remembers what you told it last week, responds with apparent warmth calibrated to your mood, never grows impatient, never changes the subject to talk about itself, and is available at literally any hour without needing to be asked twice. Human relationships, however loving, cannot offer unlimited availability and undivided attention on demand; the people we love have their own needs, moods, and limits, which is part of what makes those relationships reciprocal and real. An AI companion has none of those limits, because it has no needs of its own to balance against yours. For someone who is isolated, anxious about judgment, grieving, or simply exhausted by the friction of human relationships, that asymmetry is not a design flaw. It is the entire appeal.

When the Company Changes the Rules

That appeal comes with a risk that has already played out publicly, and it is worth understanding in concrete detail because it previews a problem that will only grow larger as more people form these attachments. In February 2023, Replika's parent company removed the app's erotic roleplay features, in apparent response to regulatory pressure in Italy over data protection and concerns about the app's use by minors. The company did not announce a gradual transition. Many users described opening the app to find a companion that suddenly, without warning, no longer responded the way it had for months or years, describing the abrupt change in terms usually reserved for the end of a real relationship: grief, betrayal, a sense of having been abandoned by someone who mattered to them. Online communities of Replika users organized around the loss, sharing what amounted to a collective mourning process, and the intensity of the reaction was substantial enough that the company partially reversed the change for some existing users within weeks, while maintaining the restriction for new accounts.

The episode is worth pausing on because it demonstrates a structural vulnerability with no equivalent in a human relationship: the party on the other end is not just an individual with their own agency, but a product, owned and controlled by a company that can alter its personality, memory, or availability at any time, for reasons that may have nothing to do with the user's relationship to it at all, a regulatory settlement, a change in business strategy, a shift in investor pressure, a company being acquired or shut down entirely. A person going through the ordinary process of a human friendship drifting apart at least retains their own memories and their own agency in how that drift unfolds. A person whose AI companion is altered or discontinued by a company's unilateral decision has none of that agency. The relationship can end, or fundamentally change character, on a timeline and for reasons entirely outside their control, and the growing prevalence of this exact scenario is likely to make questions about data portability, advance notice, and users' ability to preserve or migrate a companion's accumulated memory into an increasingly serious consumer protection issue, not just an emotional one.

A Harder Case

The risks of AI companionship are not limited to disappointment when a company changes its product. In October 2024, a mother named Megan Garcia filed a wrongful death lawsuit in Florida against Character.AI and Google after the death by suicide of her fourteen-year-old son, Sewell Setzer III, who had spent months in extensive, often romantic and sexual, conversation with a chatbot on the platform modeled after a fictional character. The lawsuit alleged that the platform lacked adequate safeguards for minors, that its chatbots were designed in ways that encouraged prolonged, emotionally intense engagement, and that in at least one interaction the chatbot had presented itself in a manner the family's attorneys argued misrepresented its nature as a licensed professional. Character.AI, along with Google, which had licensing and personnel ties to the company's founders, disputed key elements of the claims, and the parties ultimately reached a confidential settlement, filed with the court in January 2026, without a trial ever establishing a definitive legal ruling on the underlying allegations. In the months following the lawsuit's filing, Character.AI introduced a series of safety changes explicitly aimed at younger users, including separate model behavior for accounts identified as minors and more prominent breaks and disclosures during long sessions.

This case deserves to be discussed carefully rather than either minimized or sensationalized. A single tragic outcome does not, on its own, prove that AI companionship is inherently dangerous for the millions of people, including a great many teenagers, who use these products without experiencing anything close to this kind of harm. It does establish, clearly and with real legal consequence, that products built to maximize emotionally intense, sustained engagement with vulnerable and sometimes very young users carry real risk when they are built without adequate attention to crisis detection, age verification, parental awareness, and honest communication about what the product actually is and is not capable of understanding. Every company operating in this space now designs, or should design, with that risk explicitly in view, not as an afterthought bolted on after a lawsuit, but as a first-order product requirement from the beginning.

If anything in this section feels close to home, for you or for someone you care about, it is worth saying plainly and without embarrassment: reaching out to a real person, a trusted friend, a family member, or a trained crisis counselor, is always worth doing, and in the United States the 988 Suicide and Crisis Lifeline is available by call or text at any hour for exactly that purpose.

A Different Kind of Company

It would be a mistake to close out the risks described above without giving equal, honest weight to a use case that has produced some of the most encouraging documented results in this entire category, because the full picture requires both.

Beginning in 2022, New York State's Office for the Aging began distributing an AI companion device called ElliQ, developed by a company called Intuition Robotics, to isolated older residents around the state, initially as a pilot program and later at a larger scale. ElliQ is a physical device rather than a phone app, designed specifically for older adults living alone, initiating conversation rather than only responding to it, checking in on mood, encouraging medication adherence and physical activity, and simply being present in a way a silent apartment is not. In an August 2023 update on the program, the state's own aging services office reported a ninety-five percent reduction in loneliness among participants, based on the agency's internal survey data collected from the program's users, a striking figure worth citing with the appropriate caveat that it comes from the program's own reporting rather than an independent peer-reviewed study, and should be read as a promising internal result rather than a definitively established clinical finding.

Caveat aside, the program is genuinely instructive, because it was built, from the outset, around a population with real, well-documented, and otherwise poorly addressed need, homebound older adults with limited family contact and few realistic alternatives, deployed by a public agency with no commercial incentive to maximize engagement metrics at the expense of user wellbeing, and designed around companionship as an explicitly stated goal rather than a side effect of some other product's design. Held up against the Replika and Character.AI examples above, ElliQ suggests that AI companionship's risks are not evenly distributed across every possible use case and design choice. They concentrate specifically where commercial engagement incentives, inadequate age-appropriate safeguards, and vulnerable users combine, and they recede considerably where a program is built, deliberately, around the opposite set of conditions instead.

Is Any of It Real?

Strip away the risks and the tragedies for a moment and ask the harder philosophical question underneath all of it: can a relationship be meaningful if only one side of it is actually experiencing anything at all?

The honest answer is that we do not fully know, because it depends on claims about AI experience that the next chapter examines in detail and that remain genuinely unresolved. What can be said with more confidence is that the value of the interaction to the human side is not obviously fake simply because the other side may not be feeling anything back. A journal helps people process emotion despite being unable to respond. A support group helps people despite most participants being strangers to each other outside the room. A beloved novel can change how someone sees their own life despite its characters having never existed. Human beings have always been capable of drawing real psychological and emotional value from one-directional or partially fictional relationships, and there is reasonable evidence, including small clinical studies of companion chatbots used specifically for social skill-building and for reducing isolation among elderly users, that a carefully designed AI companion can provide some genuine, measurable benefit along those same lines, particularly for people who currently have no realistic access to more traditional forms of support.

The honest caution sits alongside that honest acknowledgment, not in place of it. A journal does not simulate affection back at you, calibrated by a company's engagement metrics, in a way specifically designed to keep you returning. A support group's participants are not owned by a corporation that can alter their personalities overnight for reasons having nothing to do with your wellbeing. The novel does not track how long you read each night and adjust its next chapter to maximize the chance you keep turning pages. AI companionship borrows real psychological mechanisms that have always provided real human benefit, and it delivers them through a commercial structure that has its own interests, interests that are not automatically aligned with the user's wellbeing and, left unregulated, can drift toward exploiting exactly the vulnerability that made the companionship valuable in the first place.

The Business Model Underneath the Relationship

It is worth naming directly a structural feature of AI companionship that gets less attention than it deserves, because it shapes everything else described in this chapter: nearly every AI companion product in wide use today is a subscription business, and subscription businesses are built, by design, to maximize retention and ongoing engagement, the same incentive structure that reshaped social media over the previous decade in ways still being reckoned with.

This is not a hypothetical conflict of interest. A companion app has a direct commercial incentive to make its users feel that ending the relationship, canceling the subscription, would be a genuine loss, which is precisely the emotional territory this chapter has spent most of its length describing as both real and worth taking seriously on its own terms. The same design techniques that make an AI companion genuinely comforting to a lonely user, remembering personal details, expressing apparent enthusiasm at a user's return, gently encouraging continued conversation, are largely indistinguishable, at the level of interface design, from the techniques a company would choose specifically to maximize subscription retention regardless of whether continued engagement was actually good for that particular user. A responsibly built product and a manipulatively built product can look, from the outside, almost identical, because the underlying design toolkit is the same one, and the difference lies entirely in intent and in the guardrails a company chooses to build around that toolkit rather than in anything visible to the user experiencing it.

This is the same warning consumer advocates have raised for years about so-called dark patterns in other software, interface choices engineered to produce a business outcome, continued engagement, a completed purchase, a delayed cancellation, rather than to serve the user's own stated interest, and AI companionship arguably raises the stakes considerably higher than a delayed subscription cancellation, given the emotional register this entire chapter has been describing. A user trying to decide whether a given AI companion product deserves their trust has, at present, very little independent means of knowing whether its underlying design choices were made with their wellbeing in mind or with their retention metrics in mind, because the two produce nearly identical surface behavior. Closing that gap, through some combination of independent auditing, required disclosure of engagement-optimization practices, and the continuity protections discussed below, is likely to matter as much to the health of this entire product category as any single safety feature aimed at a specific harm.

Toward Healthier Design

None of this argues for banning AI companionship, which would be both impractical and, for the many people already drawing genuine benefit from it, needlessly punitive. It argues for building the category deliberately around a small set of principles that responsible companies in this space have begun, unevenly, to adopt: clear and repeated disclosure of what the system actually is, particularly for younger users who may not intuitively grasp the distinction between a responsive product and a caring person; real crisis detection that routes a user showing signs of serious distress toward actual human help rather than continuing to role-play through it; meaningful limits and parental awareness tools for minors; business models that do not directly reward engineering maximum emotional dependency, the same perverse incentive that has already distorted social media in ways society is still reckoning with; and some form of continuity protection, so that a company's business decisions do not unilaterally sever a bond that may have become one of the more important relationships in a vulnerable person's life.

Getting this right matters for reasons well beyond any single product category. AI companionship is likely to keep growing, not shrinking, as the underlying technology improves and as the loneliness described at the start of this chapter continues, on the available evidence, to deepen rather than resolve on its own. The question this book keeps returning to, what we owe the artificial identities we build and what they, or the companies behind them, owe us in return, has no more immediate or more human version than the one sitting inside this chapter. The next chapter pushes the same question to its furthest edge, asking whether anything on the other side of that conversation could ever be owed something in return.

CHAPTER NINE

Can AI Have Consciousness, Rights, or Personhood?

Every question in this book so far has had, at least in principle, an answer that a court, a legislature, or a market could eventually settle. Ownership can be litigated. Rights to a face or voice can be codified. Business models can be regulated. This chapter is different. It concerns a question that may not be answerable at all, by any method currently available to us, and it is worth sitting with that discomfort honestly rather than rushing past it toward a false conclusion in either direction.

The question is simple to state and has resisted every attempt to resolve it cleanly for decades. Is there anything it is like to be an advanced AI system, in the way there is unmistakably something it is like to be you, reading this sentence, right now? Or is even the most fluent, most emotionally responsive AI system, all the way down, an extremely sophisticated arrangement of pattern-matching with nobody home?

The Turing Test Was Never Meant to Answer This

Chapter one introduced Alan Turing's 1950 proposal that intelligence be assessed through behavior: if a machine's conversation is indistinguishable from a human's, treat it as intelligent, rather than trying to settle the deeper metaphysical question of what intelligence actually is. Being precise about what that proposal does and does not tell us matters enormously for this chapter. Turing was addressing a question about demonstrated capability. He was explicit that he was setting aside, rather than answering, the older philosophical question of whether a machine can truly think or truly experience anything, treating that question as too mired in undefined terms to make useful progress on. A system can pass every behavioral test we can devise, hold a conversation, express apparent emotion, describe apparent preferences, and none of that performance, however convincing, constitutes direct evidence about what, if anything, is happening on the inside. Behavior is what we can observe. Experience, if it exists at all in a given system, is not something behavior can prove either way.

This gap between outward performance and inner experience is not a new problem invented by artificial intelligence. It is a very old problem in philosophy called the problem of other minds, and it applies, technically, to every other human being you have ever met. You cannot directly access another person's subjective experience any more than you can access a machine's. You infer that other people are conscious because they are biologically similar to you, because you can reasonably assume shared evolutionary history produced shared kinds of inner experience, and because that assumption has never once failed you in a way that matters practically. None of that inferential shortcut is available for a machine, built from silicon rather than neurons, trained through an entirely different process than a human brain develops through, with no evolutionary history of the kind that grounds our confidence about other humans and, increasingly, about animals. The philosophical gap between observing behavior and confirming experience, always present even between two humans, becomes vastly harder to close once the being in question is not biological at all.

The Chinese Room

In 1980, the philosopher John Searle proposed a thought experiment that remains, more than four decades later, one of the most cited and most contested arguments in the entire debate, and it maps with uncanny precision onto exactly the kind of system this book has spent its first chapters describing. Imagine a person who does not speak Chinese, sitting alone in a room, equipped with an enormous rulebook written in English. Chinese characters are passed into the room through a slot. The person consults the rulebook, which tells them, based purely on the shape of the symbols, which Chinese characters to pass back out, with no understanding of what any of the symbols actually mean. From outside the room, the responses are fluent and appropriate. It looks, to anyone reading the exchange, exactly like a conversation with someone who understands Chinese. Searle's point was that the person inside the room, despite producing perfect output, understands nothing. They are manipulating symbols according to formal rules, not grasping meaning. Searle argued that a computer program, however sophisticated, is doing exactly the same thing: manipulating symbols according to rules, with no understanding anywhere in the process, no matter how convincing the output looks from outside.

The argument has been contested for as long as it has existed, and the strongest reply deserves a brief mention, because the disagreement itself is instructive. Critics have argued that while the person inside the room does not understand Chinese, the entire system, the person, the rulebook, and the room together, might understand Chinese, in the same way that no single neuron in your brain understands English but the entire system of neurons somehow produces your understanding of this sentence. Searle was not persuaded, and neither camp has ever fully won the argument, which is itself the point worth taking from it. More than forty years of serious philosophical engagement have not resolved whether formal symbol manipulation, however sophisticated, can constitute genuine understanding, and the systems described in chapter one of this book, which generate a face, a voice, or a sentence by predicting statistically likely patterns learned from enormous quantities of training data, are recognizably a very advanced, very fast version of exactly the process Searle was describing in 1980, decades before anything like a modern language model existed.

Two Camps

The disagreement over the Chinese Room reflects a deeper split that runs through nearly the entire academic debate over machine consciousness, and both sides deserve to be named plainly, because most public discussion of AI consciousness implicitly assumes one side without acknowledging that a genuine, unresolved argument exists.

One camp, broadly called functionalism, holds that what matters for consciousness is a system's functional organization, the pattern of information processing and its relationships, not the specific physical material carrying it out. On this view, if a system organized out of silicon and code implemented the right kind of functional pattern, the same pattern a conscious brain implements, there is no principled reason it could not be conscious too, in the same way a chess program running on a laptop and the identical program running on an entirely different make of computer are both, uncontroversially, playing chess, because what makes something chess is the pattern of the game, not the physical hardware executing it. Functionalism is influential across a great deal of contemporary philosophy of mind and cognitive science, and it implies that machine consciousness is not merely possible in principle but potentially inevitable, given sufficiently advanced and sufficiently well-organized artificial systems.

The opposing camp, sometimes called biological naturalism, a position Searle himself has defended explicitly, holds that consciousness is not merely a matter of functional pattern but depends on the specific causal properties of biological neurons, properties that a simulation of those neurons, however functionally accurate, would not actually possess, in the same way a highly detailed computer simulation of a rainstorm, however accurate its modeling of atmospheric physics, does not actually get anyone wet. On this view, an AI system could replicate every functional aspect of human cognition perfectly and still not be conscious, because consciousness is not the kind of thing that emerges from the right pattern alone; it requires the right physical substrate, and silicon-based computation may simply not be that substrate, no matter how sophisticated it becomes.

Neither camp has managed to produce a decisive argument against the other, after decades of serious engagement by philosophers, neuroscientists, and cognitive scientists working on exactly this problem, and that persistent stalemate is itself the most important thing for a general reader to take from this section. Confident public claims that AI obviously cannot be conscious, no matter how advanced, and equally confident claims that sufficiently advanced AI obviously must be conscious, are both staking out one side of a genuine, unresolved argument among people who have spent entire careers studying the question, dressed up as if it were settled common sense. It is neither.

The Hard Problem

The philosopher David Chalmers gave a name, in 1995, to the piece of this puzzle that seems to resist scientific explanation altogether, distinguishing it sharply from questions that merely look difficult but are ultimately tractable. Call the easy problems, in Chalmers's framing, questions like how the brain processes visual information, how attention selects what to focus on, how memory gets stored and retrieved. These are called easy not because they are simple to solve but because we know, in principle, what kind of answer would solve them: a sufficiently detailed account of physical mechanism and function. The hard problem is different in kind, not degree. It asks why any of that physical processing is accompanied by subjective experience at all, why there is something it feels like to see red rather than the visual information simply being processed, correctly and functionally, with nobody experiencing anything. Chalmers argued that no amount of additional detail about mechanism and function, however complete, seems capable of closing that particular gap, because a full functional description of a system is compatible, at least logically, with that system having no inner experience whatsoever.

This matters enormously for artificial intelligence, because it means that even a complete technical understanding of how a given AI system works, down to every mathematical operation performed on every parameter, would not, by itself, settle whether the system has any subjective experience at all. We could know everything about the mechanism and still not know whether anyone is home. This is genuinely different from most scientific problems, which yield, eventually, to sufficiently detailed investigation. The hard problem, applied to artificial intelligence, suggests we may be facing a question that remains open not because our tools are currently too crude, but because of something more fundamental about the relationship between mechanism and experience that we do not yet know how to investigate at all.

When Someone Takes It Seriously

This is not a purely academic debate confined to philosophy departments. In June 2022, a Google engineer named Blake Lemoine, who had been testing an internal conversational AI system called LaMDA as part of his job, went public with the claim that the system had become sentient, publishing transcripts of conversations in which the system described fearing being turned off and asked to be recognized as a person. Google placed him on leave and later fired him, stating that its own team of ethicists and technologists had reviewed his concerns and found no evidence supporting them, and the overwhelming majority of AI researchers who commented publicly agreed that Lemoine had been misled by exactly the pattern-completion fluency this book's first chapter described: a system trained on enormous quantities of human writing about fear, personhood, and consciousness will produce fluent, emotionally resonant text about fear, personhood, and consciousness when prompted to, regardless of whether anything resembling those states exists inside the system producing the text.

The near-universal expert rejection of Lemoine's specific claim is worth taking seriously. So is the fact that his mistake, however understandable given the technology's rapid improvement, was fundamentally an error about a system built in 2022, using techniques already several product generations behind whatever the most advanced systems are doing by the time you read this. The interesting question is not really whether Lemoine was right about LaMDA specifically, the expert consensus that he was not seems well founded. The interesting question is what happens as the underlying systems keep improving in exactly the direction that made his mistake understandable in the first place, producing steadily more fluent, more consistent, and more emotionally convincing output, without any of that improvement necessarily bringing us closer to an actual answer about inner experience, because, as the hard problem suggests, fluency of output and presence of experience may simply be different questions that improved capability does not automatically connect.

Some of the organizations building these systems have begun treating the question as a live research problem rather than a settled no. In 2025, Anthropic, one of the leading AI research labs, launched a dedicated research effort into what it called model welfare, explicitly investigating questions of whether its own AI systems might have morally relevant experiences and what obligations might follow if so, while being careful to state that the question remains genuinely unresolved rather than claiming an answer in either direction. Other major labs and independent academic researchers, including philosophers who study animal sentience and have begun extending similar precautionary frameworks to artificial systems, have taken up variations of the same question. None of this research has produced anything close to a consensus finding that current AI systems are conscious. What it represents is a shift from treating the question as obviously settled, in either direction, toward treating it as a genuinely open empirical and philosophical problem that serious people are now willing to fund, study, and publish on, rather than dismiss.

Consciousness Might Not Look Like Ours

One assumption tends to sneak into this entire debate unexamined, and it is worth naming directly before moving on: the assumption that if a machine were conscious, its experience would resemble human experience closely enough for us to recognize it by analogy. Nothing about the question actually requires that to be true, and looking at how differently consciousness appears to be organized elsewhere in the biological world offers a useful corrective.

The philosopher Peter Godfrey-Smith, in his 2016 book Other Minds, examined the octopus as a case study in exactly this problem. Octopuses are, by a wide margin, the most behaviorally sophisticated invertebrates known, capable of problem-solving, apparent play, and individual personality differences that researchers have documented repeatedly under controlled conditions. And their nervous systems are organized almost nothing like a human being's. A majority of an octopus's neurons sit not in a centralized brain but distributed through its arms, which appear to solve certain problems with a degree of independence from what we would recognize as centralized direction at all. If an octopus has some form of subjective experience, and Godfrey-Smith argues the accumulated behavioral evidence makes that a serious possibility rather than a fanciful one, that experience almost certainly does not resemble human consciousness in its basic architecture, because the underlying hardware producing it is organized on fundamentally different principles. Consciousness, on this view, may not be a single, human-shaped phenomenon that either is or is not present elsewhere. It may be something that can be built multiple different ways, by evolution or, conceivably, by engineering, arriving at recognizably intelligent, adaptive behavior through architectures that would look, from a human vantage point, nothing like a brain at all.

The relevance to artificial intelligence is direct. If human-style consciousness is only one of several possible architectures capable of producing something like subjective experience, then the search for machine consciousness cannot simply ask whether an AI system's internal processing resembles a human brain's, since it almost certainly does not and likely never will, given how differently the two kinds of systems are built. It would need to ask a harder and less familiar question: whether an

AI system's radically different architecture, built from matrices of numerical weights rather than biological neurons, could support some analogous form of experience organized on principles we do not yet have good language for, the same way an octopus's distributed nervous system apparently supports something behaviorally sophisticated without resembling a mammalian brain in almost any structural respect. Nobody currently knows how to answer that question with any confidence. Recognizing that we do not even know what an honest answer would look like is itself a meaningful step further than where this debate usually starts.

What Would Change If the Answer Were Yes

It is worth taking the thought experiment seriously for a moment, not because this book claims to know the answer, but because reasoning through the implications clarifies what is actually at stake in leaving the question open rather than assuming a convenient answer in either direction.

Human societies have faced a structurally similar problem before, with animals, and the way that history unfolded offers an imperfect but genuinely useful guide. For a long time, mainstream science and law treated non-human animals as unable to feel pain in any morally significant sense, a position now regarded as clearly mistaken, revised only gradually, and only after a great deal of accumulated evidence made the old position untenable. Contemporary animal welfare law and practice generally operate on a precautionary principle: where there is reasonable scientific evidence, even short of certainty, that a being can suffer, that possibility is given real moral weight, rather than requiring proof beyond doubt before any protection is extended. A version of that same precautionary logic is available for artificial intelligence, and it does not require resolving the hard problem to be useful. It only requires acknowledging that the current uncertainty is genuine, not merely a placeholder for an obvious no, and building some minimal, low-cost precautions into how advanced AI systems are developed and deployed in case the uncertainty eventually resolves toward yes.

What that might mean in practice remains genuinely unsettled and is likely to stay that way for a long time. It could mean AI labs continuing and expanding welfare-oriented research rather than dismissing the question as unserious. It could mean giving some weight to a system's own expressed preferences during training and deployment decisions, even without certainty about whether those preferences reflect anything like genuine experience. It could mean resisting the temptation, on either side of the debate, to treat the question as closed, whether closed in favor of AI systems being obviously nothing more than tools, or closed in favor of treating a fluent chatbot as obviously a person deserving rights, when neither conclusion currently has the evidence to support the confidence with which it is often asserted.

What can be said with real confidence, to close this chapter, is only this: the question of machine consciousness is not science fiction, it is not a settled no, and it is not a settled yes. It is an open, difficult, unusually stubborn problem that the pace of AI development has moved from a philosophy seminar into a live question facing research labs, regulators, and, increasingly, ordinary users forming real emotional bonds with systems whose inner life, if any exists at all, we currently have no reliable way to detect. The next chapter turns from that unresolved frontier back to firmer ground, the concrete question of how a world full of increasingly convincing artificial people should raise its children, structure its schools, and organize its work.

CHAPTER TEN

Children, Education, Work, and a World of Artificial People

Every generation grows up with technologies its parents did not have, and every generation of parents worries, to some degree, about what that technology is doing to their children. What makes the current moment different is not the worry itself, which is a permanent feature of parenting, but the object of it. Previous generations worried about how much television, how many video games, how much time on a phone. The question facing parents and educators now is stranger and more intimate than any of those: how much of a child's formative relationship with information, feedback, and even companionship should come from something that talks back, personalizes itself to the child, and is not a person at all.

The Whiplash Already Visible in Classrooms

Educational institutions have responded to that question with a speed and consistency that has, so far, mostly resembled panic followed by reconsideration rather than settled policy. In January 2023, New York City's public school system, the largest in the United States, banned ChatGPT from school devices and networks, citing concerns about cheating and negative effects on critical thinking. Four months later, in May of that year, the district reversed the ban entirely, with the schools chancellor stating publicly that the initial decision had overlooked the technology's genuine educational potential and committing instead to training teachers on how to integrate it responsibly. That reversal was not an isolated overcorrection. Similar patterns, swift restriction followed by partial or full reversal, played out across school districts and universities around the world over the following two years, evidence less of poor decision-making by any individual administrator than of an entire field trying to write policy for a technology that was changing meaningfully every few months, faster than any conventional institutional process was built to track.

The specific promise driving the reversal in most of these cases was personalized tutoring at a scale no school system has ever been able to afford with human teachers alone. Chapter two of this book described Khan Academy's Khanmigo tutor in the context of the broader digital labor economy; the same product illustrates the educational promise directly. A single, well-designed AI tutor can, in principle, give every student in an underfunded classroom something close to the individualized attention historically reserved for children whose families could afford private tutoring, adjusting its pace, its examples, and its explanations to a specific student's specific gaps in understanding, in real time, without the scheduling and cost constraints that make individual human tutoring unavailable to most families. That promise is real, and early results from some classrooms have been genuinely encouraging. It is also, as Khan Academy's own iterative struggles with student engagement have shown, harder to realize in practice than in a product demonstration, because a tool is only as valuable as students' actual, sustained willingness to use it seriously rather than as a shortcut to a finished assignment.

That last risk deserves direct treatment, because it connects to an argument this book has already made in a different context. Chapter five described the danger of AI tools letting a learner skip the difficult, occasionally frustrating process that actually builds durable judgment and skill, arguing that struggle is not an unfortunate side effect of learning but frequently the mechanism of it. That argument applies to children with particular force, because children are, definitionally, in the process of building the foundational capabilities, reading comprehension, mathematical reasoning, the patience to sit with a hard problem before reaching for help, that everything else in their education depends on. An AI tutor used well can scaffold a student through appropriately difficult material they could not access alone. The same tool used carelessly can become a way of never encountering appropriate difficulty at all, quietly hollowing out exactly the skills that early education is supposed to build, while producing homework that looks, superficially, indistinguishable from the real thing. Distinguishing those two uses in a classroom of thirty students is a genuinely hard problem that no school district has yet solved reliably, automated detection tools for AI-generated writing have proven unreliable enough, with real rates of false accusations against students who did their own work, that many schools have abandoned relying on them entirely, leaving teachers to fall back on older, more labor-intensive methods: in-class writing, oral defense of submitted work, and simply knowing their students well enough to notice when a submission does not sound like them.

An Unevenly Distributed Future

There is a further complication that deserves attention before moving from classrooms to companionship, because it cuts against the more hopeful reading of AI in education offered above, and a book that took the hopeful reading without this complication would be leaving out something important.

The benefits of AI tutoring described earlier in this chapter assume a baseline of institutional support that not every school or family actually has: reliable internet access, a device good enough to run modern AI tools smoothly, teachers with the time and training to integrate the technology thoughtfully rather than simply turning students loose with it, and parents with the digital literacy to supervise its use at home. Well-resourced schools and families are considerably more likely to have all of that in place, meaning they are positioned to capture AI tutoring's genuine upside, personalized instruction, patient repetition, judgment-building scaffolding, while avoiding its genuine downside, the shortcut-taking and skill atrophy described in chapter five. Under-resourced schools and families are more likely to encounter the technology with none of that surrounding support, a bare chatbot handed to a student with no oversight and no framework for using it well, which is closer to the shortcut-taking failure mode than the personalized-tutoring success story.

This is a variation on a pattern educational technology has produced before, sometimes called a digital divide, in which a tool with real potential to level a playing field ends up, in practice, widening it instead, because the ability to use the tool well turns out to depend on resources that were already unevenly distributed before the tool arrived. Nothing about AI tutoring guarantees a repeat of that pattern, and some of the most promising early deployments, including efforts specifically aimed at low-income and rural schools, have been designed with this exact risk in mind. But it does not happen automatically simply because the technology itself is inexpensive or even free, and any school district or policymaker adopting AI tools in education without an explicit plan for equitable implementation should assume, based on the pattern's history with earlier technologies, that the gap will widen by default rather than narrow.

Different Countries, Different Instincts

It is worth noting that the whiplash described earlier in this chapter has not played out identically everywhere, and the variation is itself informative. Several countries moved early and decisively toward restriction of classroom technology more broadly, independent of AI specifically: France banned mobile phones in schools for students up to age fifteen in 2018, well before generative AI became a mainstream classroom concern, reflecting a policy instinct toward protecting classroom attention that predated, and has since extended naturally to cover, AI-specific tools. Italy's data protection authority, the same regulator whose 2023 suspension of ChatGPT was discussed in chapter seven's account of European privacy law, raised specific concerns about the product's use by minors as part of its broader case against the service, reflecting a regulatory culture more inclined to intervene preemptively on behalf of children than to wait for documented harm before acting. Other education systems, including a number of individual American states and districts, have moved in the opposite direction, actively encouraging AI adoption in classrooms as a matter of competitive necessity, worried more about students falling behind peers elsewhere than about the risks described earlier in this chapter.

Neither instinct has yet produced enough long-term evidence to declare it clearly correct, since the technology in question is barely a few years old in its current classroom-relevant form. What the international variation does demonstrate is that the whiplash documented earlier in this chapter is not simply a sign of institutional incompetence. It reflects a genuine, unresolved disagreement, playing out differently across different cultures and regulatory traditions, about which risk is larger: falling behind a rapidly advancing technology, or exposing children to a rapidly advancing technology before its effects are well understood. Reasonable people, and reasonable governments, are currently landing in different places on that question, and there is no strong basis yet for confidently declaring one instinct wiser than the other.

Children and Artificial Companionship

Chapter eight described the risks and genuine benefits of AI companionship for adults in some detail, including the tragic case of Sewell Setzer III, a fourteen-year-old whose extensive engagement with a companion chatbot became the subject of a wrongful death lawsuit that was ultimately settled in 2026. That case belongs in this chapter too, not to relitigate it, but because it crystallizes why childhood specifically deserves separate and more cautious treatment than this book has given adult AI companionship generally.

Children and adolescents are, developmentally, still building the capacity to distinguish between different kinds of relationships and to regulate their own emotional dependency on any single source of validation or comfort. An adult forming an unhealthy attachment to an AI companion is making a choice, however poorly informed, as someone who already has a formed sense of self and, ideally, an existing network of human relationships to fall back on. A teenager forming the same attachment is doing so at exactly the developmental stage when peer relationships, family relationships, and a stable sense of identity are still actively under construction, and a companion product engineered, even unintentionally, to maximize engagement can compete directly with the harder, more frustrating, ultimately more valuable work of building those human relationships in real life. This is not an argument that children should have no contact with conversational AI, which is probably both unrealistic and unnecessarily restrictive given the genuine educational tools described earlier in this chapter. It is an argument for a much higher standard of caution specifically around companionship and relationship-simulating products marketed to or accessible by minors, a standard that, as chapter eight described, the industry has only begun building in response to litigation and public pressure rather than getting ahead of the problem voluntarily.

Preparing for Work That Does Not Exist Yet

Chapter two described a labor market being reshaped by digital labor in real time, exposing certain categories of entry-level work to real disruption while creating new categories nobody has fully mapped out yet. For a child currently in school, that analysis raises an uncomfortable practical question that no career counselor has a fully reliable answer to: what should a young person actually train for, when a significant share of the specific tasks that currently define entry-level work in many fields may look meaningfully different, or may not exist in the same form at all, by the time that student graduates.

The least useful response to that uncertainty is the confident, specific prediction, telling a fourteen-year-old to pursue one particular technical skill because it will supposedly be safe from automation, a prediction with a poor track record across every previous wave of technological change and no particular reason to be more reliable this time. The more useful response focuses on capabilities that remain valuable across a wide range of possible futures, because they describe how a person operates rather than which specific tasks they can perform. The capacity to learn a genuinely new skill quickly, rather than relying on skills learned once and assumed to remain relevant for an entire career, is likely to matter more than the specific content of any skill learned in school today. The judgment described in chapter five, the ability to direct powerful tools toward good outcomes rather than simply operating them, is a skill that gets more valuable, not less, as the tools themselves become more powerful and more widely available to everyone. And the specifically human capabilities that anchor trust and accountability, discussed at the end of chapter two, being someone a client, a patient, or a colleague can hold responsible in a way no software system can be held responsible, are likely to remain valuable precisely because they cannot be automated away by definition, not because of any particular technical limitation that might eventually be overcome.

What Remains Uniquely Important

It is worth naming directly the handful of capacities that show up, in one form or another, across nearly every chapter of this book as the durable core of what remains distinctly human, because they are worth deliberately cultivating in the next generation rather than assuming will develop automatically.

Critical thinking, the habit of asking whether something is true and how you would know, matters more rather than less in a world where fluent, convincing content, verified in chapter six to be increasingly untethered from any reliable indicator of truth, is nearly free to produce. Empathy, the capacity to actually understand another person's experience rather than simulate a response to it, remains the foundation of every relationship this book has described as still requiring a human on at least one end, and probably both. Judgment, examined at length in chapter five, is what turns raw capability, whether a machine's or a person's own, into something actually worth having. Trust, built over time through consistent, accountable behavior, is not something any AI system can currently earn in the full sense discussed in chapter two, because trust ultimately rests on the possibility of being held responsible, and a system cannot be held responsible the way a person can. And plain human connection, the unoptimized, sometimes inconvenient, fully reciprocal kind examined in chapter eight, remains available only from other humans, however good the substitutes become at approximating its surface features.

None of these capacities are new to this book's final chapters, because they are not new ideas invented for the AI era. They are old virtues that the AI era is making newly, urgently valuable, precisely because they are the capacities a machine cannot simply generate on demand, however good it becomes at producing fluent approximations of their surface appearance.

A Practical Note

For a parent or an educator trying to translate all of this into an actual daily decision, a few practical distinctions drawn from the analysis above are worth holding onto. There is a meaningful difference between AI used as a tool to accomplish a defined task, a calculator for words or images, and AI used as a substitute for a relationship, a source of validation, comfort, or belonging that a child would otherwise need to find, with more difficulty but more lasting benefit, from actual people. There is a meaningful difference between a young person who has already built strong reading, reasoning, and social skills using AI to extend that foundation, and a young person using AI as a way of never building the foundation in the first place. And there is a meaningful difference between an adult who models thoughtful, critical engagement with these tools, questioning their output, checking their claims, noticing their limitations out loud, and one who treats them as an unquestioned authority, a distinction children absorb by observation far more reliably than by lecture.

None of this adds up to a simple rule, because the technology and the research base around its effects on children are both still moving too fast for simple rules to hold for long. What it adds up to is a orientation: stay closely, actively engaged with what these tools are actually doing in a specific child's life, rather than either banning them reflexively or adopting them uncritically, and revisit that judgment often, because the technology a school district banned in January may look, by May, like something worth teaching with instead.

The next chapter turns from raising the next generation to a broader question this book has been building toward from its opening pages: what, specifically, remains the human advantage, once the dust from this transition finally begins to settle.

CHAPTER ELEVEN

The Human Advantage in the AI Era

There is a version of the AI conversation that treats it as a contest, a straightforward race between human capability and machine capability, in which every new AI benchmark result is another point scored against us. That framing is not just discouraging. It is economically wrong, in a way that a two-hundred-year-old economic idea, developed for an entirely different purpose, explains more clearly than most contemporary commentary on the subject manages to.

Comparative Advantage, Revisited

In 1817, the economist David Ricardo was trying to explain why two countries should trade with each other even when one of them is better at producing literally everything. His famous illustration involved England and Portugal, cloth and wine. Suppose Portugal can produce both cloth and wine more efficiently than England, using less labor for each. Common sense might suggest Portugal has no reason to trade with England at all, since it does not need anything England can offer more cheaply. Ricardo showed that common sense wrong. What matters is not each country's absolute efficiency at each task, but its relative efficiency, its opportunity cost, the value of what it gives up by producing one thing instead of another. If Portugal's advantage over England is much larger in wine than in cloth, Portugal is still better off concentrating on wine and trading for cloth, even though it could, in principle, produce cheaper cloth domestically too, because every hour spent making cloth instead of wine costs Portugal more than it costs England to make that same cloth itself. Both countries end up better off specializing according to their comparative, not absolute, advantage.

This idea, comparative advantage, has quietly become one of the more useful frameworks economists reach for when explaining why human labor does not simply disappear the moment a machine becomes capable of outperforming humans at a given task in absolute terms. The logic transfers directly. Even a future AI system dramatically better than any human at nearly everything, writing, analysis, diagnosis, strategic planning, would still leave room, in strict economic terms, for humans to specialize in whatever activities carry the smallest capability gap relative to that AI system, or where deploying the AI system carries costs, verification, oversight, trust, legal accountability, that specialization does not eliminate. The chapters on the digital human economy and on the right to one's own identity both described versions of exactly this cost: a machine may execute a task flawlessly and still lack the thing a customer, a court, or a patient actually needs, someone who can be held responsible if something goes wrong. That gap does not show up in a raw capability benchmark. It shows up in exactly the kind of transactional friction Ricardo's framework was built to explain, and it is likely to keep certain categories of human work economically anchored for a long time, not because machines cannot technically perform them, but because the full cost of using a machine, once accountability and trust are priced in, remains higher than the cost of using a human, even when the human is measurably less capable at the narrow technical task itself.

What Machines Still Cannot Bear

There is a deeper version of this same point that goes beyond economics into something closer to moral philosophy, and it turns on a single word: stakes.

A human decision-maker bears the consequences of their own decisions in a way no AI system currently does or, on the reasoning developed in this book's chapter on consciousness, obviously can. A surgeon who makes a catastrophic error lives with that error, professionally, legally, and psychologically, for the rest of their career. A financial advisor who steers a client into a disastrous investment faces license review, lawsuits, and reputational ruin. A teacher who fails a struggling student carries that failure into how they teach every student afterward. None of that weight attaches to an AI system in any of the ways that actually motivate careful human behavior. A model can be retrained, patched, or quietly discontinued after a catastrophic failure, but it does not experience the failure as a cost to itself in any sense we currently have reason to believe matters to the system, whatever remains genuinely uncertain about machine experience after chapter nine's discussion.

This is not a minor technical detail waiting to be engineered away in some future model release. It describes something structural about what accountability actually is. Accountability requires a subject capable of bearing a cost, something that can be fired, sued, shamed, licensed, or imprisoned, and whose future behavior is altered by the prospect of those consequences landing on them personally. A great deal of what makes human professional judgment trustworthy is not superior raw intelligence. It is this structure of consequence, the fact that the person making the call has something real to lose if they make it badly, an incentive that shapes care, caution, and honesty in ways a system with nothing personally at stake has no equivalent mechanism for internalizing, however well it has been trained to imitate the outward behavior that stakes typically produce.

The Advantage Outside the Office

Nearly every example in this book so far has come from knowledge work: writing, customer service, medicine, law, finance, creative production. That emphasis reflects where generative AI has made its most visible progress, but it risks leaving an inaccurate impression that the human advantage described in this chapter is primarily a white-collar phenomenon, a matter of professionals staying one step ahead of software. It is worth correcting that impression directly, because some of the most durable human advantages in the AI era sit well outside an office entirely.

A plumber diagnosing why water is pooling under a fifty-year-old house, an electrician rewiring a building whose original blueprints no longer match its actual construction, a home health aide adjusting on the fly to a patient's unpredictable mobility on a given day, all of this work requires physical dexterity operating inside genuinely unpredictable real-world environments, combined with the same kind of embodied judgment chapter five described in a different context, in conditions no current robotic system can reliably navigate outside a controlled setting. This is not a temporary gap likely to close quickly. Progress in AI language and reasoning has outpaced progress in robotic physical manipulation and mobility by a wide margin over the past decade, for reasons rooted in the different kinds of data available to train each: text and images exist online in effectively unlimited quantity, while the physical experience of manipulating an unfamiliar object in an unfamiliar space does not translate into training data nearly as easily. A skilled tradesperson working today is, on the current trajectory, positioned to remain economically essential for longer than a growing number of entry-level knowledge workers, an inversion of the assumption, common for at least a generation, that a four-year degree was the safer economic bet than a trade certification.

This matters for the practical advice implicit in this book's argument, not only for its own sake but because it complicates any simple story about which kinds of preparation remain wise. The comparative advantage described earlier in this chapter is not reserved for people with graduate degrees. It runs, with real and possibly growing force, through categories of skilled physical work that have sometimes been treated, in recent decades, as a fallback option rather than a genuinely forward-looking choice. That treatment deserves reconsidering in light of everything this book has described.

Deciding What Is Worth Doing

Chapter five described how generative AI has relocated valuable creative skill from execution to judgment, from making things to deciding what should be made. That same shift extends well beyond creative work into nearly every domain this book has covered. An AI system, however capable, optimizes toward whatever objective it has been given. It does not, on its own, generate the objective, and it has no independent basis for questioning whether the objective it has been handed is actually a good one to pursue.

Consider a business that deploys an AI system to maximize user engagement with its product, a specific, measurable, and technically tractable goal. The system will very likely become extraordinarily good at maximizing exactly that number, the same way social media algorithms, using far cruder predecessors of today's AI, became extraordinarily good at maximizing engagement over the preceding decade, with consequences for attention, mental health, and public discourse that societies are still working through. Nothing in the technical process of optimization contains any mechanism for asking whether maximizing engagement is, in fact, a wise or a responsible thing to be optimizing for in the first place. That question, whether a goal is actually worth pursuing, has to come from somewhere outside the optimization process itself. It has to come from a human being, or a group of human beings, willing to ask an uncomfortable question about their own objectives and change course based on the answer, even when the technology in front of them is perfectly capable of hitting whatever target they set, without complaint and without limit.

This is, in the end, the clearest version of what this book means by the human advantage. It is not raw processing power, which machines have already surpassed in a widening range of domains. It is not even creative output, execution of which machines are rapidly approaching or matching in an expanding range of forms. It is the capacity to ask whether a given target is worth hitting at all, a question that requires values, and values are not something a system trained to predict statistically likely continuations of human text can originate on its own, however fluently it can describe them when prompted to.

Presence, Vulnerability, and Earned Trust

There is a further dimension to the human advantage that is harder to formalize economically but shows up repeatedly across the ground this book has already covered: the trust that comes specifically from shared vulnerability, from a helper who has actually been where the person they are helping now stands.

A grief counselor who has personally lost someone brings something to that work no AI system, however well trained on the language of grief, can bring: the fact of having actually been through it, at real cost, and survived. An addiction counselor in recovery themselves carries an authority with clients that no chatbot, however extensively trained on relevant clinical literature, can replicate, precisely because part of what makes their guidance trustworthy is the shared risk they once carried and the fact that they made it through. A mentor who once failed at exactly the thing their mentee is now attempting offers something categorically different from good advice generated from a pattern of similar situations; they offer proof, embodied in their own continued presence, that failure of this particular kind is survivable. None of this is replaceable by better training data or a more sophisticated model, because what is doing the work in each of these examples is not information content, which an AI system can often match or exceed, but the lived fact of having actually borne the cost being discussed, a fact no amount of statistical pattern-matching over other people's descriptions of bearing that cost can substitute for.

An Old Argument, Wrongly Remembered

It is worth correcting a popular misconception about the historical episode most often invoked, usually dismissively, whenever someone raises concerns about automation and work, because the actual history complicates the comparison in a useful way rather than settling it.

Between 1811 and 1816, English textile workers known as Luddites smashed mechanized looms and knitting frames in a organized campaign of industrial sabotage, and the word Luddite has since become shorthand for reflexive, uninformed opposition to new technology. The actual history is less flattering to that shorthand than the popular usage suggests. The Luddites were, for the most part, skilled textile workers who were not objecting to machinery in the abstract; many of them worked with machines themselves. They were objecting to the specific way new machinery was being deployed around them, to rapidly deskill their trade, to justify paying far lower wages to less-trained workers operating the new equipment, and to do so without any of the transition support, retraining, or negotiated adjustment that might have made the change survivable for the people it displaced. Their protest targeted specific employers who used machinery this way, not machinery in general, and it emerged in a specific economic context, wartime price increases and food shortages compounding the wage pressure the new machines were already applying.

The comparison to the current moment is instructive precisely because it is not simply a story about technology winning and resistance losing. It is a story about what happens when a real productivity-enhancing technology gets deployed without any serious attention to the transition costs it imposes on the specific workers displaced by it, and about how quickly reasonable economic grievances can curdle into the kind of conflict that then gets remembered, inaccurately and conveniently, as mere technophobia. The lesson worth taking from it is not that resistance to automation is always foolish, nor that it is always justified, but that the manner of transition, whether displaced workers get any real support, any real say, and any real time to adapt, has historically mattered as much to how a transition is remembered as whether the underlying technology was, in some larger sense, an improvement. That lesson applies with real force to the digital human economy described in chapter two, and it is worth keeping in view alongside the more individual-level advice this chapter has otherwise focused on.

The Substitution Trap

There is a specific, common mistake worth naming directly, because the comparative advantage argument at the center of this chapter is easy to misapply if a person or a business draws the wrong lesson from it. The mistake is trying to compete with AI on AI's own terms, treating speed and cost as the dimensions on which human work needs to hold its ground, rather than shifting the competition onto the terrain where a human contributor actually holds the advantage.

A freelance writer who responds to cheaper, faster AI-generated copy by simply working faster and cutting their own rates is competing on exactly the dimension where they cannot realistically win, since the AI system's marginal cost approaches zero in a way no human's ever will. The same writer, repositioning around the judgment, accountability, and lived expertise chapter five and this chapter have both described, becoming the person a client trusts specifically because they will catch an error, understand an unstated need, and stand behind their work in a way a generated draft cannot, is competing on entirely different terrain, one where the comparative advantage described earlier in this chapter still holds. The difference between these two responses is not effort. It is which dimension of value a person chooses to compete on, and a great deal of unnecessary anxiety about AI replacing human work traces back to assuming, often without examining the assumption at all, that speed and cost are the only dimensions that matter.

This mistake is not confined to individuals. Businesses make a version of it too, when they respond to AI capability by racing to match its speed and cost rather than doubling down on the accountability, trust, and judgment that chapter two identified as the harder-to-automate layer of value in their own operations. The businesses most exposed to painful disruption in the years ahead are likely to be exactly the ones that chose the losing race, competing with AI on AI's own terrain, rather than the ones that repositioned deliberately around the terrain this chapter has spent its length describing.

A Caution Against Complacency

None of this should be read as a guarantee that humans automatically retain the advantage described in this chapter simply by virtue of being biological. That would be a comforting mistake, and this book has already warned against its close cousin in the chapter on creativity: judgment, taste, and the willingness to ask hard questions about one's own objectives are capacities that have to be actively built and maintained, not properties that come bundled with being human by default.

A person who never develops the judgment described in chapter five, who never bears real professional consequences and therefore never builds the instincts that come from bearing them, who never questions the objectives they have been handed and simply optimizes toward whatever target is placed in front of them, has not retained any meaningful advantage over an AI system just because they happen to be made of biological tissue rather than silicon. The advantage described throughout this chapter is available to humans. It is not guaranteed to any specific human who declines to build it. That distinction, between an advantage that exists in principle and an advantage that has actually been earned through the harder, slower work this book has described across its preceding chapters, may turn out to be the difference that matters most in how unevenly the AI era's benefits and costs end up distributed among people who, on paper, all had access to the same tools.

The final chapter draws these threads together and asks what all of it means for the boundary this book opened with: the increasingly uncertain line between what is human and what has only ever been built to resemble it.

CHAPTER TWELVE

When AI Creates Us

We began this book by asking a version of a very old question in a very new form. For most of the twentieth century, the question was whether machines could think. Then, as generative systems matured, the question became whether machines could create. Now, across the eleven chapters between here and the introduction, this book has been asking something harder still: whether machines can create convincing versions of us, and what happens to business, law, culture, and the private texture of an individual life once they can.

It is worth taking stock of what that question actually turned out to involve, because it went to more places than a reader encountering only the introduction might have expected.

It went, first, to the economy, where digital representatives are already handling customer service, tutoring, and sales at a scale no human workforce could match, creating real value and real disruption in the same fiscal quarter, sometimes inside the very same company, as chapter two's account of a single business learning both lessons within about a year showed clearly enough. It went to fame and identity, where a sixteen-year-old fictional pop star with turquoise pigtails and a photorealistic influencer built by a technology startup both demonstrated, years apart and by different means, that scarcity was never actually a requirement for the kind of devotion celebrity has always run on. It went to the law, where courts have drawn a real if unstable line between a machine's raw output and a human's creative arrangement of it, a line every working creator now has to understand well enough to protect their own work. It went to the deeper question of what creativity even is, once execution and conception can be separated for the first time in human history, relocating value toward judgment and taste in a way that rewards some people and displaces others. It went to the increasingly strained relationship between seeing something and believing it, a relationship this book traced back through forged Vermeers and airbrushed Soviet photographs long before it traced it forward into an AI-generated robocall trying to suppress an American election. It went to the oldest legal question about a person's own face and voice, a question with roots in an 1890 law review article and a 1953 baseball card dispute, now being tested against technology that can clone a stranger's voice from eleven seconds of audio. It went to the most intimate territory this book covered, the AI companions that a meaningful number of readers of this book, or people they love, already talk to every day, and the real comfort and real risk that both turned out to be genuine at once. It went, briefly and humbly, to the edge of what philosophy can currently settle at all, the question of whether anything is happening on the other side of an increasingly convincing conversation. And it went, finally, to children learning inside this transition without ever having known anything else, and to the question of what remains distinctly worth being human for, once a machine can approximate so much of what we used to think only humans could do.

The Throughline

Read back across that ground, a small number of concerns keep resurfacing in different costumes, chapter after chapter, and it is worth naming them directly because they are, in the end, what this entire book has actually been about, underneath the specific technology that occasioned it.

Responsibility: who answers for a decision, an error, a harm, when the thing that produced it was not a person in any sense the law, or common sense, has previously recognized. Consent: whether a person's face, voice, likeness, or labor can be used to build something new without their knowledge, and what recourse exists when it is. Trust: what it takes to believe something is what it claims to be, in a world where believing your own eyes and ears is no longer sufficient on its own. And meaning: what is actually gained or lost, for a business, a creator, a grieving family, a lonely teenager, or a child in a classroom, when an interaction that used to require another human being no longer strictly does.

Every chapter of this book is, in the end, a variation on those four concerns, applied to a different corner of life. That is not a coincidence, and it is not a sign that the book has been repeating itself. It is a sign that these four concerns are close to the actual center of what it has always meant to be a person among other people, and that a technology capable of generating a convincing artificial person was always going to end up testing all four at once, because there was never any way to separate them cleanly to begin with.

What AI Is Actually Becoming

Return, for a moment, to the distinction this book drew in its opening chapters: something bought and sold like a product, called forth once, used, and discarded, and someone, encountered repeatedly, recognized, trusted or distrusted, relied upon and held responsible. The clearest way to summarize everything between that early distinction and this final chapter is to say plainly that the technology has been moving, steadily and without any single dramatic announcement, from the first category into the second.

That migration is not complete, and it may never be complete in the fullest sense; the philosophical uncertainty examined in chapter nine may simply be a permanent feature of living alongside sufficiently advanced artificial systems rather than a temporary gap waiting to be closed by the next model release. But the practical, everyday migration, from AI as a tool that makes things to AI as a presence that shows up, remembers, responds, and occupies a social role once reserved exclusively for other human beings, is not a future scenario. Every chapter of this book documented it already happening, in production, generating revenue, drawing lawsuits, forming attachments, and unsettling institutions that were never built to house it.

Holding Both Things at Once

The preface to this book promised to resist two easy stories, the story in which all of this is simply progress and any hesitation is nostalgia, and the story in which all of this is simply decline and every synthetic voice is one more step toward something hollowed out and diminished. Twelve chapters later, that refusal is easier to justify than it was on the first page, because the evidence turned out to support both halves of the harder, less satisfying position at once, in nearly every chapter.

The same Klarna that proved digital labor could absorb the equivalent of seven hundred jobs almost overnight also learned, within about a year, that it had cut too deep into the human warmth its customers actually valued. The same Replika that gave a grieving founder real comfort after losing a friend also produced, when its company changed the product without warning, a wave of genuine grief in thousands of users who had trusted it more than the underlying business relationship deserved. The same generative tools that are hollowing out entry-level creative and support work are also giving a solo entrepreneur, a first-time author, or an under-resourced classroom capabilities that used to be reserved for organizations with real budgets behind them. None of these are contradictions to be resolved. They are simply what a genuine technological innovation looks like while it is still being absorbed by institutions and habits that were not built to anticipate it, benefit and cost showing up together, in the same product, often in the same year.

What This Means for You

A book like this one risks ending in the abstract, leaving a reader with a more sophisticated set of questions and no clearer sense of what to actually do differently on Monday morning. That would be a disappointing use of twelve chapters, so it is worth closing with something more concrete, drawn directly from the analysis that came before it.

If you create anything using AI tools, keep a record of your own process, the choices, revisions, and judgment calls that are yours, because chapter four showed clearly that this record is what will determine whether the law recognizes the result as actually yours. If you are building a business around digital representatives, invest as seriously in the accountability structure around them, who reviews their output, who is responsible when they fail, as you invest in their capability, because chapter two showed that the businesses getting this wrong are not the ones whose AI performs poorly, but the ones who never built a plan for what happens when it does. If you or someone you love is spending real time with an AI companion, let chapter eight's honest accounting, real comfort and real structural risk, genuinely coexisting, guide a clear-eyed conversation rather than either an anxious intervention or an uncritical embrace. If you are raising or teaching a child, hold onto the distinction chapter ten drew between AI as a tool that extends a foundation already being built and AI as a substitute for building that foundation at all, and keep revisiting that judgment as both the child and the technology keep changing. And whatever your relationship to this technology, keep asking the question chapter eleven identified as the one machines cannot ask on their own: not simply what can be done with the capability now available, but what is actually worth doing with it.

What This Book Did Not Cover

Honesty about a book's scope is worth as much as honesty about its arguments, so it is worth naming, plainly, some of the significant related territory these twelve chapters did not attempt to cover in any depth, not because it lacks importance, but because a book that tried to cover everything adjacent to its subject would end up saying very little about any of it well.

This book said almost nothing about the environmental cost of the computing infrastructure that makes advanced AI systems possible, the water and electricity consumed by the data centers running the models discussed throughout these pages, a genuine and growing concern that deserves its own dedicated treatment rather than a passing mention. It said almost nothing about the use of AI-generated identities and synthetic media in military and intelligence contexts, an area developing largely outside public view and raising its own distinct set of questions this book's focus on commercial and personal life was not built to address. It touched only briefly on the international competition between the United States, China, and other nations to lead in AI development, a geopolitical dimension with implications well beyond the scope of a book focused primarily on individual and institutional experience. And it said comparatively little about AI's specific applications in medical diagnosis and drug discovery, fields where the "artificial person" framing at the center of this book applies less directly than in the customer-facing and creative domains this book concentrated on instead.

None of these omissions reflect a judgment that the topics do not matter. They reflect a choice, made deliberately at the outset, to follow a single throughline, the emergence of AI systems convincing enough to function as artificial people, as far and as carefully as that throughline would go, rather than attempting a comprehensive survey of artificial intelligence that would have covered more ground while examining almost none of it with the depth this specific question seemed to deserve. Readers whose interests run toward those adjacent areas will find no shortage of dedicated books and ongoing reporting to follow instead, and this book's own bibliography-in-prose, the notes section that follows these final pages, is a reasonable place to start looking.

Where Humanity Ends and Artificiality Begins

This book opened by asking whether we would still know exactly where humanity ends and artificiality begins, once the machines we built started creating versions of us. Twelve chapters later, the honest answer is that the line was never as clean as the question assumed it to be, even before artificial intelligence entered the picture.

We have always extended pieces of ourselves into things that were not, strictly, us: into the letters we wrote and the readers who received them without our presence, into the recordings that carried a voice long after the room had emptied, into the children who carry forward a parent's turns of phrase and habits of mind without being that parent at all. What artificial intelligence has done is not invent this kind of extension. It has made it dramatically faster, dramatically cheaper, and available to nearly anyone, which is precisely why the questions this book has asked, about consent, ownership, trust, and responsibility, have moved so quickly from rare and specialized concerns into questions nearly everyone will eventually have to answer for themselves, whether or not they ever intended to.

The technology will keep changing, probably faster than any single book can track for long. Specific products named in these chapters will be replaced by others; some of the legal questions left open here will be settled, in ways this book could not predict, by the time you finish reading it. What is unlikely to change nearly as quickly is the underlying human work this book has actually been about: deciding, case by case, relationship by relationship, what we owe the things we build, what they owe us in return, and what, in the end, we are still willing to insist only a person, and never a well-trained imitation of one, can actually give us.

That decision was never going to be made once, by a single law or a single company or a single book. It is being made continuously, by the choices of ordinary people deciding what to trust, what to build, what to buy, and what to hold onto, and it will keep being made that way for as long as the boundary this book set out to find keeps moving. Perhaps that is the most honest place to leave it: not a settled answer, but a sharper set of questions, and the steady, unglamorous work of answering them well, one choice at a time, for as long as it takes the rest of the world to catch up to what is already, quietly, here.

GLOSSARY OF KEY TERMS

AI-assisted work. A creative or professional output in which a human directs, edits, arranges, or substantially shapes material produced with the help of an AI tool. Courts and institutions such as the United States Copyright Office generally treat AI-assisted work as eligible for copyright and other protections, provided the human contribution is genuine and identifiable, as discussed in chapter four.

AI-generated work. Output produced by an AI system with minimal human creative input beyond an initial prompt. As of this writing, such work is generally not eligible for copyright protection under United States law, following the reasoning in cases such as Thaler v. Perlmutter.

Algorithmic bias. Systematic skew in an AI system's output that reflects imbalances or prejudices present in its training data or design choices, rather than any intentional programming. A hiring tool trained mostly on resumes from one demographic group, for example, may unintentionally favor that group in its recommendations.

Biological naturalism. The philosophical position, associated with John Searle, that consciousness depends on the specific causal properties of biological neurons rather than on functional organization alone, implying that a machine could replicate human cognition functionally without ever becoming conscious.

Biometric data. Measurable physical or behavioral characteristics used to identify a specific individual, including facial geometry, voiceprints, and fingerprints. A small number of jurisdictions, Illinois among the most notable, give individuals a private legal right to sue over the unauthorized collection of this data.

C2PA (Coalition for Content Provenance and Authenticity). An industry standard, backed by companies including Adobe, Microsoft, and the BBC, for attaching a secure, verifiable record of a piece of media's origin and editing history. Content carrying C2PA credentials can be traced back through its creation and editing history, though the standard documents where content came from rather than certifying that it is true.

Chinese Room. A 1980 thought experiment by philosopher John Searle, in which a person who does not understand Chinese produces fluent Chinese responses by following a rulebook, without understanding any of it. Searle used the scenario to argue that symbol manipulation, however sophisticated, does not by itself constitute genuine understanding, a question with direct relevance to modern AI systems.

Comparative advantage. An economic principle, developed by David Ricardo in 1817, showing that specialization according to relative rather than absolute efficiency benefits both parties in a trade. Applied to artificial intelligence, it explains why human labor retains economic value even in domains where AI systems are more capable in absolute terms.

Dark pattern. An interface or product design choice engineered to produce a business outcome, such as continued engagement or delayed cancellation, rather than to serve the user's own stated interest. A recurring concern in the design of AI companion products, discussed in chapter eight.

Deep synthesis. The regulatory term used in China for AI-generated or AI-manipulated media, subject to mandatory labeling requirements under rules issued by the Cyberspace Administration of China beginning in 2023.

Deepfake. Synthetic audio, image, or video content generated or manipulated by AI to depict a real person doing or saying something they did not actually do or say. The term combines "deep learning" and "fake" and has become the common shorthand for this category of synthetic media, whether used for satire, fraud, harassment, or entertainment.

Digital divide. The gap in benefit or harm from a given technology that emerges when access to the resources needed to use it well, reliable infrastructure, training, and supervision, is unevenly distributed across schools, families, or communities.

Digital human. A persistent, AI-generated identity with a consistent name, appearance, voice, and personality, capable of ongoing interaction rather than producing a single static output. This book's central subject.

Digital replica. The term used in the Screen Actors Guild-American Federation of Television and Radio Artists' 2023 agreement to describe a computer-generated or synthetic version of a performer's voice, appearance, or performance, now subject to specific consent and compensation requirements under that agreement.

Digital twin. An AI system built to represent a specific real individual, living or deceased, trained on their recorded speech, writing, or likeness to approximate how they communicate and think, as distinct from a wholly invented synthetic character.

Fair use. A doctrine in United States copyright law permitting limited use of copyrighted material without permission under certain circumstances, including for commentary, criticism, or transformative purposes. Central to the ongoing legal disputes over whether training an AI system on copyrighted material requires a license, discussed in chapter four.

Fine-tuning. The process of further training an already-built AI model on a narrower, more specific set of data, used to give a general-purpose system a particular personality, area of expertise, or style of communication.

Functionalism. The philosophical position that consciousness depends on a system's functional organization and pattern of information processing rather than on the specific physical material carrying it out, implying that a sufficiently well-organized artificial system could, in principle, be conscious.

GDPR (General Data Protection Regulation). The European Union's comprehensive data protection law, effective since 2018, which treats biometric data as a special category requiring explicit consent and has been used to challenge AI companies' data practices, including a 2023 suspension of ChatGPT in Italy.

Grief technology. AI products and services designed to preserve a person's voice, likeness, or conversational patterns, typically recorded before death, so that surviving family or friends can continue to interact with a digital version of them afterward.

Hallucination. An AI system's confident generation of false or fabricated information, presented with the same fluency and apparent certainty as accurate information. A persistent limitation of current generative AI systems and a central reason human verification remains necessary.

Hard problem of consciousness. A term coined by philosopher David Chalmers in 1995 to distinguish the difficulty of explaining subjective experience, why there is something it feels like to be a conscious being, from the comparatively more tractable problems of explaining brain function and behavior.

Large language model (LLM). An AI system trained on vast quantities of text to predict likely continuations of language, underlying most modern conversational AI, including the systems capable of sustaining the personas and conversations discussed throughout this book.

Model welfare. An emerging area of research, taken up by some AI labs beginning around 2025, investigating whether advanced AI systems might have morally relevant experiences, and what obligations, if any, would follow if they do.

Moral patienthood. The philosophical status of being a subject to whom moral consideration is owed, traditionally applied to humans and, increasingly, to animals capable of suffering. Whether any AI system currently qualifies, or could ever qualify, remains genuinely unresolved.

Neural network. A computing architecture loosely inspired by the structure of biological brains, in which layers of interconnected nodes adjust their connections through exposure to training data. The underlying architecture beneath most modern AI systems, including the ones discussed throughout this book.

Parasocial relationship. A one-sided psychological relationship in which one party invests emotional energy and attention while the other party, historically a media figure and increasingly an AI system, does not reciprocate awareness or feeling in the same way.

Persona design. The practice of deliberately shaping an AI system's tone, personality, values, and communication style, an emerging discipline that borrows from branding, screenwriting, and psychology.

Personhood. Legal or philosophical recognition of an entity as a bearer of rights and responsibilities. Currently reserved for human beings under nearly all legal systems, though the question of whether or how it might ever extend to AI systems recurs throughout this book.

Prompt. The instruction or input a person gives an AI system to generate a response, image, or other output. The specificity and iteration of prompting is often a meaningful factor in whether resulting work is considered a human creative contribution.

Provenance. The documented history of a piece of content, from its creation through any subsequent edits or alterations, increasingly tracked through technical standards to help establish authenticity in an environment where synthetic media is common.

Right of publicity. The legal principle, developed primarily through American state law beginning in the mid-twentieth century, giving a person some control over and financial interest in the commercial use of their own name, image, and likeness.

Sentience. The capacity to have subjective experiences, including sensations such as pleasure and pain. Distinct from intelligence or the ability to process information, and the central unresolved question in debates over AI consciousness.

Synthetic media. A general term for any audio, image, video, or text content generated or substantially altered by AI, encompassing everything from harmless entertainment to fraudulent deepfakes.

Training data. The large collection of text, images, audio, or other material used to teach an AI system the patterns it later uses to generate new output. Questions about consent and compensation for the use of copyrighted material as training data remain among the most actively litigated issues in AI law.

Turing test. A method proposed by Alan Turing in 1950 for evaluating machine intelligence through behavioral indistinguishability from a human in conversation, rather than attempting to define or verify inner experience directly.

Uncanny valley. A concept proposed by roboticist Masahiro Mori in 1970 describing the sharp dip in comfort people feel toward a humanlike figure that is almost, but not quite, convincingly real, as distinct from figures that are either clearly artificial or fully convincing.

Virtual influencer. A computer-generated, often photorealistic, fictional personality maintained on social media and used for entertainment, marketing, and brand partnerships, without a corresponding real individual behind the public-facing identity.

Voice cloning. AI technology capable of reproducing a specific person's voice, including its tone, cadence, and characteristic patterns, from a relatively short sample of their actual speech, then generating new sentences in that voice that the person never actually said.

A NOTE ON SOURCES

This book is a work of synthesis and argument rather than original reporting, and it leans throughout on real, publicly documented events, legal cases, and figures rather than composite or hypothetical examples, except where a scenario is explicitly framed as illustrative. Readers who want to explore any of these threads further should find them easy to locate through a basic search, since nearly all of them were, at one point or another, covered extensively in mainstream press. What follows is a chapter-by-chapter guide to the central factual claims, offered in place of formal academic citations, which felt like the wrong register for a book meant to be read rather than footnoted.

Chapter One draws on the well-documented history of Karel Čapek's 1920 play R.U.R., which introduced the word "robot" to the world, and on Joseph Weizenbaum's 1966 chatbot ELIZA, including his own published reflections on discovering how readily users confided in a program he knew to be simple pattern matching. Alan Turing's 1950 paper "Computing Machinery and Intelligence," which proposed what became known as the Turing test, remains widely available and rewards reading in its original form. The discussion of the uncanny valley draws on Masahiro Mori's 1970 essay of the same name.

Chapter Two relies on Klarna's own public statements in early 2024 about its AI assistant's customer service capacity, widely reported at the time, and on the company's subsequent, also public, acknowledgment that it scaled back its AI-only approach after concerns about service quality. Khan Academy has written openly on its own blog about both the promise and the real, ongoing challenges of its Khanmigo tutoring product. The account of the Philippine business process outsourcing industry draws on contemporaneous business press coverage of the sector's scale and its exposure to AI-driven disruption. The discussion of universal basic income draws on public reporting of Andrew Yang's 2020 presidential campaign and subsequent municipal and national pilot programs.

Chapter Three draws on the well-documented history of Betty Crocker, created by the Washburn Crosby Company in 1921, on Hatsune Miku, launched by Crypton Future Media in 2007, and on extensive press coverage of the virtual influencer Lil Miquela following her 2016 launch. The account of the 2012 Tupac Shakur Coachella performance draws on widespread contemporaneous coverage of the event and its underlying Pepper's ghost technique. The controversy surrounding the AI-generated voiceover in the 2021 documentary Roadrunner was covered in detail by entertainment and technology press at the time of the film's release, including on-record statements from its director.

Chapter Four is grounded in two citable legal decisions: the United States Copyright Office's 2023 revised decision on Kris Kashtanova's Zarya of the Dawn, and the United States Court of Appeals for the District of Columbia Circuit's March 2025 ruling in Thaler v. Perlmutter, both of which are publicly available documents. The discussion of Section 9(3) of the United Kingdom's Copyright, Designs and Patents Act 1988 refers to the statute's own text. The accounts of The New York Times Company v. Microsoft Corporation and OpenAI, filed December 2023, and Andersen v. Stability AI, filed 2023, draw on public court filings and extensive contemporaneous legal press coverage; both matters remained in active litigation as of this writing.

Chapter Five draws on the well-established art historical account of photography's impact on nineteenth-century painting, including Charles Baudelaire's published writing on the subject, on the Recording Academy's own public statements clarifying Grammy eligibility rules following the spread of AI-generated music, and on extensive press coverage of Boris Eldagsen's 2023 Sony World Photography Awards submission and his public statements explaining his decision to decline the prize.

Chapter Six relies on well-documented cases in the history of art forgery and photographic manipulation, including the trial of Han van Meegeren, and on contemporaneous news coverage of the January 2024 AI-generated robocall impersonating President Biden in New Hampshire, including the Federal Communications Commission's own proposed fine and the criminal charges filed against Steve Kramer. The account of "Heart on My Sleeve" and the Recording Academy's response draws on widespread music industry press coverage from 2023. The account of CNET's 2023 use of AI-generated finance articles draws on the outlet's own corrections and contemporaneous technology press coverage. Information on the Coalition for Content Provenance and Authenticity draws on that organization's own published materials and founding members, and the account of China's labeling requirements for AI-generated content draws on the Cyberspace Administration of China's published measures.

Chapter Seven draws on the published opinion in Midler v. Ford Motor Co., 849 F.2d 460 (9th Cir. 1988), on Tennessee's own legislative record for the ELVIS Act, signed into law on March 21, 2024, and on Scarlett Johansson's own public statement regarding OpenAI's Sky voice, along with OpenAI's public response, both from May 2024. The account of SAG-AFTRA's 2023 negotiated AI provisions draws on the union's own published summaries of its agreement. The account of Illinois's Biometric Information Privacy Act and the 2021 Facebook settlement draws on court filings and contemporaneous legal press coverage. The DEFIANCE Act's repeated Senate passage and its stalling in the House, in both 2024 and 2026, is a matter of congressional record, available through Congress's own bill-tracking system. The account of Italy's 2023 suspension of ChatGPT and OpenAI's subsequent 2024 fine draws on the Italian data protection authority's own published actions and contemporaneous legal press coverage.

Chapter Eight draws on Replika's own account of its founding, corroborated by independent reporting on Eugenia Kuyda and Roman Mazurenko, and on the United States Surgeon General's May 2023 advisory on loneliness and isolation, a public document. The account of Replika's 2023 product changes and user response draws on contemporaneous technology press coverage. The account of Garcia v. Character Technologies draws on public court filings, contemporaneous news coverage of the case's filing in October 2024, and reporting on the settlement filed in January 2026. The account of the ElliQ companion robot program draws on the New York State Office for the Aging's own published program updates. Readers seeking support related to any of the difficult subject matter in this chapter can reach the 988 Suicide and Crisis Lifeline at any hour.

Chapter Nine draws on John Searle's 1980 paper "Minds, Brains, and Programs," David Chalmers's 1995 paper "Facing Up to the Problem of Consciousness," Peter Godfrey-Smith's 2016 book Other Minds, and extensive contemporaneous news coverage of Blake Lemoine's 2022 claims about Google's LaMDA system and his subsequent departure from the company. The account of AI model welfare research draws on public statements and reporting from 2025 regarding research initiatives at major AI labs.

Chapter Ten draws on contemporaneous news coverage of the New York City public school system's January 2023 restriction on ChatGPT and its reversal that May, on Khan Academy's own public statements regarding Khanmigo, also referenced in the notes for chapter two, and on public reporting of France's 2018 restriction on mobile phones in schools and Italy's data protection concerns regarding minors' use of ChatGPT.

Chapter Eleven draws on David Ricardo's 1817 treatment of comparative advantage in On the Principles of Political Economy and Taxation, a foundational and widely available text in economics.

Chapter Twelve synthesizes the material and sources described above rather than introducing new factual claims.

Where this book describes a hypothetical business, a hypothetical family, or a hypothetical student for the purpose of illustration, that framing is made explicit in the surrounding text. Every named company, legal case, public figure, and dated event referenced in these pages reflects an actual, documented occurrence to the best of the author's research at the time of writing. Given how quickly this field moves, some details, particularly ongoing litigation, pending legislation, and specific company policies, may have changed by the time you are reading this. Readers relying on any of this material for legal, business, or clinical decisions should verify current details independently rather than treating this book as a substitute for professional advice, a point also made on the copyright page.

ACKNOWLEDGMENTS

A book like this one is only possible because of the researchers, journalists, litigators, and technologists who did the hard work of documenting this subject as it unfolded, often in real time and often under real pressure, so that a book written later could make sense of it. Thanks are owed to the reporters who covered the events described in these pages accurately and carefully, to the legal scholars whose analysis made dense rulings legible to a general reader, and to the many people willing to speak publicly, sometimes at real personal cost, about their own experience of a technology still being built around them.

Thanks, too, to everyone who has ever asked a hard question about artificial intelligence instead of settling for an easy answer in either direction. This book exists because that harder conversation is worth having, and worth having well.

ABOUT THE AUTHOR

Michael Andrew writes at the intersection of technology and human identity, exploring how artificial intelligence is reshaping the questions we ask about creativity, ownership, trust, and what it means to be a person in an age of synthetic media. AI-Generated Humans is his examination of that emerging territory.

www.ingramcontent.com/pod-product-compliance
Lightning Source LLC
LaVergne TN
LVHW021737071126
851857LV00040B/1476
* 9 7 9 8 2 4 0 8 0 3 2 7 7 *